DRAWN THREE WAYS

Drawn Three Ways

Memoir of a Ministry,
a Profession,
and a Marriage

A. E. Harvey

WILLIAM B. EERDMANS PUBLISHING COMPANY

GRAND RAPIDS, MICHIGAN

Published 2016 by
Wm. B. Eerdmans Publishing Co.
2140 Oak Industrial Drive N.E., Grand Rapids, Michigan 49505

Printed in the United States of America

22 21 20 19 18 17 16   7 6 5 4 3 2 1

Library of Congress Cataloging-in-Publication Data

Names: Harvey, A. E. (Anthony Ernest), author.
Title: Drawn three ways: memoir of a ministry,
a profession, and a marriage / Anthony Harvey.
Description: Grand Rapids, Michigan: Eerdmans Publishing Company, 2016.
Identifiers: LCCN 2015050828 | ISBN 9780802873323 (pbk.)
Subjects: LCSH: Harvey, A. E. (Anthony Ernest). |
Church of England — Clergy — Biography. |
Theologians — Great Britain — Biography.
Classification: LCC BX5199.H367 A3 2016 | DDC 283.092 — dc23
LC record available at http://lccn.loc.gov/2015050828

www.eerdmans.com

Contents

Foreword

Anthony Harvey has been, in a variety of quiet but deeply effective ways, a profound influence in the life of the Church of England. As a scholar, a teacher of ordination candidates and many others, a writer who has illuminated biblical topics and connected them with current theological concerns, and a pastor of acute sensitivity, he has helped to form generations of intelligent clergy and engaged laypeople. He shows clearly that an "academic" ministry is anything but a detached one. An abiding and articulate care for the forgotten and neglected, for migrants and detainees, for those struggling with poverty in central Africa and those struggling with inflexible religious institutionalism nearer home, has been a constant thread in his ministry. From his involvement in the groundbreaking report *Faith in the City* and its implementation in the 1980s to more recent interventions in national and international issues, he has maintained a resolute independence and moral clarity, at the service of those who are most inconvenient to tidy-minded and nervous authorities.

This moving and unpretentious memoir charts a journey of education in faith, not least through times of deep challenge in personal life. It shows us a scholar always willing to put the resources of a remarkable learning at the disposal of the Christian community. His life story is a testimony to a style of Anglican identity that seems in some danger of being eclipsed these days — intelligently critical, sharply aware of the contradictions of being a minister of the gospel at the heart of establishment (canons of Westminster are not exactly marginal people, but they are in a remarkably good position to offer space for the marginal to speak and be visible), absorbed in the creative business of allowing Scripture to speak in a complex social environment without resorting to intellectual or imaginative shortcuts. It is a timely picture of what the Church of England can still be at its best.

But the weight and force of the book come from his honesty in charting "triumphs" and "failures" alike, with clarity and without self-pity or self-dramatizing. This is not only the record of a theological "career," but a genuine confession of faith. It has the capacity to rekindle faith in the theological vocation in the fullest sense of the word "theological," and to renew a confidence in the possibility of interweaving human honesty and Christian depth. It is a timely book and I feel privileged to have read it.

ROWAN WILLIAMS

Preface

I have often been asked in recent years whether I would think of writing an account of my life, particularly of my time at Westminster Abbey, where I was canon and sub-dean for seventeen years and certainly witnessed and participated in occasions that are worth recording from the point of view of a privileged observer and participant. But I doubted whether the rest of my life held sufficient interest to any but my friends and family to be worth submitting to a wider readership. When I began to reflect on it, I found that the various and varied phases of my journey — teaching and research in a university, training clergy, carrying out pastoral duties — were held together by a number of influences and motivations that were worth exploring in their own right, and that my abilities and my character — as well as my faith, which I sense has evolved from that of a stoic Christian to that of a Christian Stoic — had developed over time in ways that might be interesting to others outside my immediate circle. And there was a further motive. I had married Julian, a person of remarkable talents, including a gift for vivid prose and evocative poetry, some of which I longed to make available to a larger public. It seemed that a record of my own life might provide a framework within which some examples of her work could be made known. Accordingly I have sought to integrate these elements in a narrative of our life together.

I was fortunate to receive advice and acute criticism from Marge Clouts, a person of long experience and expert literary judgment.

Without her encouragement the book might never have been completed. To her I owe profound gratitude. But she carries, of course, no responsibility for any errors of judgment and taste that the book may contain. I am also deeply grateful to my family and friends who have given me loyal support on my journey along the three ways that I felt drawn to follow, and have striven to combine, during the greater part of my life.

ANTHONY HARVEY
January 2016

Timeline

CHAPTER 1

A Gifted Amateur?

When I was at Oxford as an undergraduate around 1951 I had a tutor for ancient history who was, even by the standards of the day, unusual. Each student was obliged to arrive precisely on the hour, neither earlier nor later. As the clock struck, one knocked at the door and was invited to come in by a voice that seemed to come from some inner room, where perhaps a cup of coffee had been brewing. After sitting down and reading out one's weekly essay one was asked to go and sit at a small table and take down the tutor's words verbatim. So I found myself obediently writing such sentences as, "The weakness of Mr. Harvey's argument is ..." His eccentricities extended even to delivering his lectures at dictation speed, such was his distrust of the ability of undergraduates to take correct notes of his carefully weighed historical judgments. Yet he was a highly respected ancient historian and in many ways an excellent tutor. On one occasion I had come up with what I thought was an ingenious theory, suggesting that Thucydides had been mistaken in his account of a certain battle and that I could work out myself what had really happened. "You know, Mr. Harvey," he said with a sardonic smile, "if you tear up the only evidence we have you can say anything you like, and it won't be worth saying." He then looked at me over his spectacles and remarked, not unkindly, "I suppose, Mr. Harvey, you are really just a gifted amateur." The phrase stuck in my mind, and my life has not belied it. It has been one of the threads woven into the texture of my career as an academic theologian, a priest of the Church of England, and an occasional contributor to public discussion of ethical and political issues.

Gifted? Early in life, certainly, some gifts were showing; the amateur began to show later. My school career at Eton was no more than moderately successful academically, though I had the rare distinction of seeing my name on the Honors boards for no less than three musical instruments in the same year — piano, violin, and organ. A consequence of this was that after leaving school, where I had obtained a scholarship to Oxford (at the second attempt), I spent a year in Brussels, studying the violin under a wonderful teacher at the Conservatoire, Maurice Raskin. My contemporaries in 1948 were being called up to National Service, but I was judged by the army to be in the very lowest category of fitness due to a major operation on my leg when I was five, and so was given a perfunctory dismissal. What should I do instead? My father had recently got to know some Belgian cousins of his in Brussels. Among them was Marguerite de Callataÿ, the grand-daughter of the sculptor Thomas Vinçotte, who created the fine statue of King Leopold (who is wearing what looks at first sight like a long dressing gown) that stands outside the Palais Royal. He also made the quadriga and horses that surmount the Arc de Triomphe in one of the parks, and some exquisite smaller sculptures that can be seen in museums. Marguerite herself was by any standard an exceptional woman. She and her husband (formerly in the Belgian air force) had been in the Resistance throughout the war. They had heroically continued to make contact with the Allies through a radio set hidden in a basket under the mushrooms they were ostensibly gathering, and had escaped capture despite being publicly sentenced to death for many months. They now lived in the center of Brussels where there was a substantial family network, and my parents felt confident in sending me into their care. It would be an opportunity to learn French and acquire some proficiency on a musical instrument.

Marguerite and her husband Vincent (they had no children) lived in the center of Brussels, but their flat was not large enough to have me as a permanent lodger, so I had to look for my own lodgings. The problem was to find any that would tolerate a lodger who was going to practice the violin in his room for up to eight hours a day. In the end I found a lodging house run by a scruffy Belgian woman. She lived with a Russian émigré, who evidently beat her at night (we could hear screams from below stairs) but who was liable to appear at breakfast the next morning as the very image of a cultured and civilized man, ready to instruct me about Lermontov, Pushkin, and other Russian writers about whom, at that stage in my life, I naturally knew nothing. In those days I had a fried egg for my breakfast, and I guess it was her dubious cooking procedures that induced an attack of acute anemia and constipation, such that when I returned home at Christmas, gaunt and ill nourished, my mother was not at all pleased: she had expected our cousins to keep an eye on me more effectively. But meanwhile I had introduced to the house another young Englishman who was also studying the violin at the Conservatoire, but under André Gertler, so that any other residents had to endure two violins playing simultaneously for many hours of the day. Later on I moved to a house further from the center that was quieter and more salubrious. This was a typical bourgeois family, with whose seventeen-year-old son Michel I became friends. They were comfortably off, and their style of life was characteristic of the Belgian bourgeois culture. When I asked Michel about guests they had to meals, he replied, "Oh, we never have anyone but relations or people doing business with us." When I remarked that in England we were used to having a more hospitable table, he replied, "Ça doit coûter cher à la fin de l'année," "That must become expensive by the end of the year." Indeed I experienced this myself on both sides of the line, so to speak. Being within a Belgian family network, I was frequently invited to meals; from those with whom I had no family contact, no invitation ever came.

I arrived in Brussels in September 1948 as a singularly raw and inexperienced young man. In my childhood I had been kept very firmly at home: a major operation on my leg for osteomyelitis (it was before penicillin was used to treat infections) meant I was confined to bed for six months when I was five in a Swiss clinic (the disease had attacked me when I was in Switzerland for TB glands — the mountain air was thought to be the best antidote at the time). When I could be brought home I was firmly taken to the house my parents had bought in the country, and kept at home for lessons until at the age of nine I was thought fit enough to go as the only day-boy to a local preparatory boarding school — and physically I must have been, since I had to bicycle some two miles through the woods to get there, wartime petrol rationing making other means impossible. Only when I was eleven did my mother reluctantly consent to me becoming a boarder at the Dragon School in Oxford (where my father had been a pupil himself and then a governor), and here I was rapidly brought up to the level required to get a scholarship (low down the list) to Eton. Even there I was still relatively cosseted: I endured the inevitable school boy ridicule when I was required to have a rest on a bed every day after lunch (sometimes not even allowed to read, though I managed to evade the prohibition quite often), and holidays were always spent at home — it was, after all, in wartime and in the years of rationing and austerity that followed the war.

Thus I was quite unprepared to make my own way in a foreign city on the meager allowance that government currency regulations permitted at the time. I remember walking back from the Conservatoire looking for somewhere to have lunch and finding nowhere except an obviously expensive and fashionable restaurant. I went in and sat down. Confronted by the sumptuous menu, in my school boy French I ordered the cheapest thing I could find, a tiny starter of smoked salmon, for which I paid the waiter and then, with acute self-consciousness (and unabated hunger), left the room under his cynical gaze. It was only then that I realized that I would have to swallow my pride in my own very limited savoir faire and ask some other students where to go to find something to eat I could afford. But the episode illustrates a trait which persisted in my character for many years. I had an intractable urge to demonstrate my independence. I wanted to show that I could manage without help from others, that I already knew what they could tell me and that I could get away with the appearance of superior experience and knowledge. If, in conversation, I was asked if I had read a certain book, I found myself answering "Yes," even if I hadn't, for fear of seeming less well educated. If I was trying to find my way through a strange town I would prefer to crouch discreetly over a map rather than ask for help from a passer-by (I could not bear being thought of as an "ordinary tourist"). When I visited France after learning some French in Brussels I hoped that my accent would make people think I was Belgian rather than discover the truth that I was no more than an English innocent abroad. Hence my reluctance even to ask where I should go for lunch. This was perhaps the negative side of the slightly arrogant self-confidence which Eton tended to give to us, and which indeed I found repugnant in my fellow Old Etonians and was ashamed of in myself. By going off on my own to play the violin in Brussels I naively thought I was making a break with the Etonian culture from which I now wanted to dissociate myself.

Certainly, the impact that Brussels made on me was dramatic. Coming from the darkness and austerity of London, where there was still strict food rationing, a ban on all but necessary street lighting and advertisements, drab clothes (skirts of wartime length, short to save cloth), and little traffic, the sense of abundance and prosperity was extraordinary — all made possible, people said, by the wealth of what was still the Belgian Congo. Bakeries' shelves were loaded with luscious cream cakes (to which the figures of many Belgian women bore testimony), meat — so scarce in Britain — was consumed in generous portions, and the streets were brilliant with neon light signs. There was one in particular that I could see from my bedroom, flaming against the sky. It had the four letters only, FIAT, which my classical education led me to interpret immediately as the Latin word meaning "Let it come to pass!" At that time I knew nothing about Italian cars, and so I naively assumed it was a kind of statement of confidence by the Belgian people. It chimed in with my excitement at all this new experience being offered me. I was ready to make the most of it. Yes, let it come to pass!

On my first day I presented myself for auditions at the Conservatoire. I had offered two instruments, piano and violin, expecting the piano to be my main one, since I had already acquired a reasonable technique, whereas on the violin I was still quite tentative. It chanced that the first audition was for the violin. Maurice Raskin, the violin professor conducting the auditions, listened to me, commented audibly to his colleagues that I had chosen a difficult piece (or else that he had to make a difficult decision — I just heard the word "difficile"), but must have seen something promising in me, since he accepted me straight away into his class, recommending a book of elementary exercises to get me going on my daily stint of six hours' practice. No one said anything about the piano: it turned out that the concept of a second instrument, taken for granted in British music colleges, was unknown at the Conservatoire. The consequence was that, had I been accepted for the piano, I might have been brought up to somewhere near the standard for a professional career; pure chance had placed me under Raskin's expert and attentive care, but this could do no more than equip me as a very average amateur. Which is not to say that I did not gain a great deal of pleasure and satisfaction from it, both in the long hours of rigorous practice in Brussels and in all the music making I was able to do afterwards. I had been gifted enough to secure a fine teacher and to experience learning an instrument with professional discipline, but I emerged, predictably, with no more than a moderate capability.

But I did learn to speak French with some fluency, and this prompted an urge to test and improve it in a genuinely French environment. I had discovered that speaking a foreign language seemed to lessen some of the inhibitions that I had developed during a public school education and made me feel a subtly different and less pretentious person; so I yearned to spend more time where I could pick up genuinely French idioms and manners. I also still needed to prove my independence and self-reliance. When the Conservatoire closed for the summer I hitch-hiked to Namur, took a tourist boat up the Meuse as far as the frontier, and then walked all the way to Geneva — or so I claimed afterwards, though in fact I "cheated," or rather avoided monotony, by accepting a lift with a commercial traveler across the flat plains of Lorraine. The walk took me through the beautiful rolling hills of the French Ardennes, past the battlefields and ruined fortifications of several European wars. I slept in tiny hotels or private houses among welcoming French peasants and artisans, who greeted me all the more warmly when I finally confessed I was English and not (as they thought at first) Belgian: they had seen virtually no foreign visitors since the Allied armies had passed through and were only too pleased to welcome a representative of the liberators, however young and insignificant.

After the Ardennes came the Jura, where I met a young Englishman doing exactly the same thing, also about to go up to Oxford. We walked together for a few days and then parted by mutual consent, each perhaps feeling the same need to make our own way on our own terms. For the final descent into Geneva I was offered a lift with a French charcutier and his family, who introduced me to the splendors of a French bourgeois picnic. First we stopped at a café for an aperitif, then we found a spot in the country where the full panoply could be disposed — a table and chairs, large pans full of cold water where butter, cheese and fruit were kept fresh, an immense choice from the *patron's* own charcuterie, several fresh baguettes, salad, and a gorgeous fruit tart bought from the local bakery, with wine and bottled water in abundance. Thus treated to the very best their culinary culture could offer, they courteously drove me to within a few miles of Geneva, where I arrived in such exhaustion after many weeks' walking that I went straight to sleep in the first modest inn I could find, despite a deafening noise from the bar where some Swiss locals were singing boisterously to an accordion. Next day I took the train back to Brussels, and so to London.

There my parents were waiting for me with some anxiety. They had had to endure a complete lack of contact with me for a month, apart from an occasional postcard depicting little-known views of the French countryside. And it was not an easy time for them. We had last been together (apart from my brief visits home at Christmas and Easter) when in the summer of 1948, just after I left school, we had a family holiday in a long boat on the Dutch canals. At least we would have done, had it not been for the catastrophe that overtook us after just a few days. My sister Jean, four years older than I was (I had no other brothers or sisters) had joined us from Germany, where she was serving in the Control Commission with the F.A.N.Y.'s. She had enlisted in this rather exclusive women's corps when she was eighteen, had followed our armies up through Italy until VE Day, then been posted to the Far East until the end of the war with Japan, and finally to Germany, where she had wonderful scope for indulging her ruling passion — not shared by me at all — which was horses and show-jumping. She came on leave to Amsterdam and joined us on the boat. A few days later she complained of what seemed like the 'flu. My father, an intensely energetic man then in his forties, persuaded her that the best antidote would be a brisk walk, and set off with her through the meadows. Next day she could not get out of her bunk. She had got the dreaded poliomyelitis, exacerbated by her physically strenuous life in Germany and then, tragically, by the ill-judged exercise with my father the day before. We rapidly steered the boat back to Amsterdam, and moored close to a hospital where she was cared for until she could be flown back to England. She was still in the Nuffield Hospital in Oxford when I returned a year later, the doctors struggling to give her back some use of her limbs below the waist. In the end they succeeded in enabling her to walk with crutches, which she continued to do for the rest of her life with extraordinary willpower. But that first year had not been an easy time for my parents to have the added anxiety of an inexperienced eighteen-year-old son adrift beyond recall in rural France.

Things started to go well once I got to Oxford. I had gained a scholarship to Worcester College, at that time still not thought to have much distinction other than its beautiful buildings and garden, but staffed by a group of brilliant young dons who had arrived shortly after the war and worked enthusiastically together to make the college a genuinely formative and stimulating place for its undergraduates. For my first two years I had a tutor who was not of this ilk at all, an older man whose methods were those of a schoolmaster more than of a university teacher, and who subjected us to severe and monotonous discipline. Some of his pupils were too discouraged to continue classical studies, but I found I was learning a valuable precision and accuracy from his pedagogic methods, and I was also enthused by the teaching I received in my "special subject" (Greek Lyric Poetry) from a German professor, exiled by the Nazis before the war, who gave me an insight into what real scholarship meant. I went on to achieve a double first in Mods and Greats (classics, ancient history, and philosophy) and, having apparently done the best philosophy paper in finals, was confidently expected by my philosophy tutor (who should certainly take most of the credit for my good degree) to end up as at least as head of a college. What astonishes me now is that I had such academic success on top of so much else: rowing for my college for the first year or two, doing a great deal of music, producing and directing an opera with some well-known professional singers (who obligingly lent their services to me, a mere third-year student and musical amateur), acting Jacques in *As You Like It*, and being president both of the University Music Society and of the college Junior Common Room — all time-consuming occupations. Maybe the physical and mental coordination required to play a musical instrument with such persistence for a year had sharpened up my intellect. I believe others have noticed the same. At any rate, my academic performance was such that a university career was there for the asking. Oxford in those days had an unashamed preference for its own graduates when making appointments, and I was aware there were high expectations of me.

The first step was some post-graduate study, preferably abroad. I had of course done a little travelling during my time at Oxford. Several times I was irresistibly drawn to Paris, but once I took advantage of an invitation to stay in Athens and had the privilege of visiting the major sites in Greece before the tourist industry had got going after the war. While in Brussels I had kept my body fit by joining a squash club, where I met Henry, a Greek of my own age with whom I ostensibly had little in common (his father had made a fortune in marine insurance and Henry had similar interests and priorities) but with whom I formed quite a close and lasting friendship. I was invited to join him for a holiday in his parents' home in 1950, at a time when the civil war had just ended and prisoners were still being brought in armed vans to the police station that was opposite their house in Plaka, an old quarter of Athens. From there I set out on my explorations. The only transport consisted of the buses used by the country people, which came into Athens early in the morning and left late in the evening; so to visit any site more than a few miles away one had to spend at least two nights there in little hotels that were still barely accustomed to receiving any guests at all.

These conditions brought out the innate hospitality of Greek country people to an extraordinary degree, and they never allowed my faltering Modern Greek, my ignorance or my nervousness to damp their concern that I should be properly housed and fed. On one long bus journey across the Peloponnese to Olympia I found that a halt had been made at midday (I had no idea how long the journey through the mountains was going to take) and I was firmly escorted from the bus and made to share the meal at the *taverna* that the other passengers were enjoying. It was a privilege to be seeing the great monuments of the classical age entirely alone, surrounded by the unaffected warmth of the Greek people. On one occasion I was walking in the mountains and was suddenly surrounded by three fierce and angry sheepdogs. I tried to make a slow and conciliatory retreat, but one of them snapped at my leg and bit me. At that moment the shepherd appeared, drove the dogs off me by pelting them with stones, and took me at once, with many apologies, to the tent where he was living. His wife, equally concerned, took a wad of cotton wool, dipped it in some yellow liquid, held it in the tongs, put it into the embers of the fire and then thrust it immediately on to my leg. The pain, for a few minutes, was intense, but I realized she had cauterized the wound and probably saved me from rabies. More apologies again and explanations that I only partly understood about the need to have fierce dogs to protect the sheep (I imagine from wolves). The episode confirmed my admiration and respect for the Greek people who had heroically survived the ruthless Nazi occupation and kept their innate courtesy and considerateness intact. It should also have been a timely warning against roaming the Greek mountains without taking precautions, but it regrettably failed to cure me of my reluctance to reveal my ignorance and inexperience by asking anyone's advice before setting out.

Before leaving Oxford I had obtained a university travelling scholarship which enabled me to spend two years abroad, and in the autumn of 1953 I drove my second-hand Morris 8 through France to Germany to work on Sappho, Alcaeus, and the other Greek lyric poets at the feet of Rudolf Pfeiffer, my revered Oxford teacher. A scholar of great distinction (though his only major publication, his magnificent critical edition of Callimachus, was not published until some years later), he had been given refuge from Nazi Germany in an Oxford college until he was able to return to Munich to take up the chair he had held until shortly before the war — his wife was partly Jewish. I had been fortunate to have some German lessons from the wife of a refugee dentist, who lived near our home in Buckinghamshire and with whom I also played string quartets. Nevertheless I was still shockingly unprepared to fend for myself. I arrived in a student lodging house already bursting with boisterous Bavarian students much younger than myself and offering the inmates accommodation at alarmingly close quarters with each other. Within an hour I had fled, not only, I fear, because I could not face the physical and social conditions, but because I had formed an image of myself as a superior postgraduate who simply did not belong to the rough and tumble world of first-year students.

Fortunately I had an introduction in my pocket to an English couple, who generously took me in at an hour's notice and allowed me to stay until I had found more appropriate lodgings. Of these I had several during the two years I spent in Munich, the last of which became an important part of my German experience. The head of the family was a historian of science who ran the museum of the history of science. He had been in Sweden throughout the war and was relatively innocent of its horrors. His wife, in the 'thirties, had been a member of the "over forties club," a group of women who had all had a late child because they believed that Hitler was making Germany at last a country really worth living in. Neither of them was in any sense a Nazi, indeed they had undergone a considerable reaction from the Nazi period, but I could learn from them some inklings of what it would have been like to be an independently minded but not openly antagonistic citizen before and during the war, and I came to respect them for their evident integrity. They had of course been aware that something was going on at Dachau, an extermination camp only a few miles away, but had always thought it prudent not to ask questions, and I realized I could hardly criticize them for that, given the caution they were forced to show at the time.

Another reason why I valued my time with them arose from the living conditions in Munich, which prevailed for some years after the war. Much of the city was still in ruins — the Opera, the Pinakothek, most of the museums — and housing was scarce. Private individuals were not allowed to have empty spare rooms. Accordingly every house had multiple occupation, and kitchens were shared. This meant that formal hospitality such as dinner parties was impracticable, and evenings with friends took the form of coffee and a glass of wine. Hence a degree of informal hospitality that made social contacts unusually easy and relaxed, and I had many opportunities of getting to know my landlords, their friends and other chance acquaintances. Among these was an American married couple with whom I formed the first really intimate friendship of my adult life. Robert was doing research into medieval history — he subsequently became a distinguished historian — and his wife Joan had strong literary interests. At that stage in their lives they were deeply in love with each other, and they adopted me into intimacy with them without any apparent ruffling of their own intense relationship or of my own sensibility. It was only much later, after the birth of their one child, that I heard they had caused each other acute pain; I had a fifteen-page closely typed letter from Robert, and later on Joan, who had fled into hiding and taken another name, wrote an autobiographical novel about it. But in Munich they became close and steady friends. I was a constant visitor to their flat and we spent many hours exploring together the wonderful Bavarian rococo churches. It meant, among other things, that I had friends whom I could lean on in the coming great emotional experience of my life.

It was in my last months abroad — the summer of 1955 — that I did my travelling. I had made sure I chose a subject for research which involved consulting manuscripts in the most desirable places in Europe (important manuscripts of Athenaeus, one of the sources for my research, were conveniently in Florence and Venice). Accordingly I prepared myself to drive my little old car over the Alps. Part of my preparation was reading Heinrich Heine's ironically romantic account of his journey from Munich to Genoa in 1828, and I experienced much of the same excitement, and indulged (I suspect) in similar romantic fantasies, as the grey mountain weather gave way to clear Italian skies and the green hats and leather clothing of the mountain people were replaced by the flowing skirts of girls who in those days rode side-saddle behind their boyfriends on Vespas. In my car I had of course travelled three times as fast as Heine in his stage coach, but I arrived in Trento, the first truly Italian town after the still German-speaking Tyrol, just as he did, late in the evening, and walked in amazement among the shadowy dilapidated buildings, revelling in the sense of historical continuity back to Roman times which old Italian cities offer in their very stones. Then over the Apennines into Florence, where I visited the British consulate for a formal introduction to the Laurentian Library.

While standing at the reception desk I noticed a contemporary of mine, once at school with me, trying to get from a secretary the telephone number of his godfather in Florence so as to call on him before he left. The secretary was saying all the correct things about not being able to reveal telephone numbers, "but if you like to leave a letter we'll see it gets there" — which of course was no use under the circumstances. At that moment a small man with a pronounced limp appeared, overheard the conversation and broke in: "Of course I know your godfather. Let's ring him up straight away." It was only later that I realized he was the consul, and a most unusual one at that. He seemed seldom to be in his office, but preferred roaming the building and chatting with visitors. Yet he was evidently effective and efficient. He was allowed to remain in this, his first and only diplomatic post, for a full nine years — a position coveted by consular professionals and normally held for not more than three. During his time he not only transformed the consulate into a wonderfully harmonious and personal British/Italian team; he also formed a close friendship with the mayor of Florence, the visionary and ascetic, deeply Christian and philosophically Marxist, Giorgio La Pira. The two of them became among the best known and (at least in the consul's case) most revered public figures in Florence for a number of years.

As a result of this unusual informality I was soon in conversation with the consul and found myself invited up to their house — a villa overlooking the city — for tea. There I met Julian, and there began the first and only serious experience of romantic love in my life — there had been a brief flutter when I was eighteen in Brussels, which had quickly petered out, and I went through Oxford with no emotional stirrings at all. Hence it found me totally and naively unprepared and resistant. If her father, Ian McMaster, was an unusual person, her mother Jane was even more so. She was a scholarly historian before she married (she became a fellow of the Royal Historical Society), a brilliant artist with her pencil (backs of menus were covered with vivid sketches of fellow diners, lecture notes wreathed with marginal sketches), a consummate dressmaker (she had sat up right through the night to make a dress for Julian's "coming out" presentation at Buckingham Palace), and a competent manager of a household which, in Florence, involved frequent official entertainments, yet with a manner that was startlingly unconventional, playful, and seemingly vague. Indeed, both of them abruptly enlarged my notions of how normal conventions and expectations could be subverted with benign consequences, and I revered them both for the rest of their lives.

As for Julian, here was another completely new experience. I can capture some of my feelings at the time through a letter I wrote to Joan in Munich:

> Can one fall in love with a fairy? With a creature whose mind, full of poetry, curiosity and rich experience, flits from one thing to another with Ariel speed, leaving me panting behind, wondering whether I dreamt it? With a creature so elusive that I don't merely not understand, I don't know what questions to ask. It is like talking to a beautiful, gentle wild animal that, when you put out your hand, frolics unaccountably away....

That encounter alone was enough to create some emotional turmoil. But shortly after I returned from Florence to Munich I was startled by receiving a letter from Julian's father inviting me to join them at a conference on Elba to do with psychical research. It emerged that an elderly Englishman, who had retired to Florence after making a fortune from Sicilian Marsala, experienced regular intimations from the "Beyond" or the "Above" at noon every day, and had convened a conference in a hotel he owned on the island, inviting a mixed and in many cases distinguished group of people to discuss such phenomena. This included a famous medium, a well-established Swiss theologian, a retired Swedish ambassador, and a number of others of the same caliber. Would I be interested? Hardly my field of interest, and normally I would have declined. But Julian would be there ... And when I duly arrived on the ferry, I was greeted by her parents without a trace of surprise as if I was already a regular and welcome visitor.

I tried to convey some impression of this extraordinary gathering in the same letter to Joan:

> I suppose it is not surprising that I should feel a little out of water among thirty or forty people whose interests are spiritualism, theosophy, psychic phenomena or some related subject for which I have always entertained a healthy scepticism (as it is, my sense of humour is overworked).... They are of every type: saints, scholars, sages, cranks and careerists, but all friendly, willing to talk, sincere, rather happy. Every meal is an adventure in a strange territory, every cup of coffee may be enriched with an astonishing anecdote. It all gives one an unusual freedom: one may make almost any statement or profession of belief and expect to be listened to without surprise. If I were to claim to be a lion-tamer investigating the survival of the souls of beasts after death I feel I should be accepted with just as much readiness as I am when I pose as a scholar or a philosopher or whatever role seems most appropriate at the time. This kind of irresponsibility is perhaps part of the enchantment: my normal self is not an important part of my luggage. And the warm lotus beauty of Elba lulls to sleep any scruples which remain.

What followed was like a sequence from a romantic film script. Julian and I were both billeted in a private house near the hotel, in rooms one above the other (deliberately? I never knew). The setting was idyllic, our evening walks together of astounding beauty, the company in the hotel intriguing, the sense of being already part of the family yet another new experience. So much so that immediately my puritanical soul began to protest. After all these years when I had felt no sexual or romantic urges, was I now being cast in the part of a lover? Was this me at all, or was I simply acting out a role which circumstances (possibly with help from Ian and Jane) had thrust on me? Was I genuinely in love, or was I simply acting out the part appropriate to such a dream-like setting? And when, after my return to Munich for the final few days of my time there, I began to write her long letters, the debate within myself that I tried to explain to her was all to do with "honesty": had I just been playing the role of lover in a setting that seemed laid out for the part in an almost theatrical mise-en-scène, or was I genuinely in love? I was obsessed with the dishonesty I would have been guilty of had I been only playing a part. My internal debate went on at varying degrees of intensity for many months after that, and involved poor Julian in an answering uncertainty. Yet all the signs were there of a deepening attachment, which was finally sealed by our marriage in 1957.

I find my state of mind at this time strikingly paralleled in a poem by Robert Browning, *Two in the Campagna*. He describes the birth of mutual affection among the flowery ruins outside Rome:

> I wonder do you feel to-day
> As I have felt since, hand in hand,
> We sat down on the grass, to stray
> In spirit better through the land,
> This morn of Rome and May?

The experience (so like mine in Elba) left the poet attracted, tantalized, unsure of himself, but with an unquenchable yearning:

> I would I could adopt your will,
> See with your eyes, and set my heart
> Beating by yours, and drink my fill
> At your soul's springs, — your part my part
> In life, for good and ill.

A Gifted Amateur?

No. I yearn upward, touch you close,
    Then stand away. I kiss your cheek,
Catch your soul's warmth, — I pluck the rose
    And love it more than tongue can speak —
Then the good minute goes.

Already how am I so far
    Out of that minute? Must I go
Still like the thistle-ball, no bar,
    Onward, whenever light winds blow,
Fixed by no friendly star?

Just when I seemed about to learn!
    Where is the thread now? Off again!
The old trick! Only I discern —
    Infinite passion, and the pain
Of finite hearts that yearn.

CHAPTER 2

Julian

S ince this memoir is about Julian as well as about me, it is time to
say more about her gifts and character, and to draw on some of
her own recollections. She had an astonishing memory (at least compared with mine) for her experiences in early childhood; indeed she
seemed to have an uncanny familiarity with things that happened
even before she was born (or rather a highly retentive memory of her
mother's own vivid descriptions). Her mother, after reading history
at Somerville College, Oxford, had gone to do research on the Duke
of Hamilton's papers in Edinburgh, and was staying with the family
of Sir Herbert Grierson, a notable scholar of English literature. There,
among others, she met W. B. Yeats, and evidently charmed him. The
episode, as recounted by her mother, from many years before she was
born, evidently lodged itself so firmly in Julian's memory that, many
years later, she was able to write a vivid account of it, that gives not
only a taste of Jane's character but a picture also of Edinburgh in the
early 1920s.[1]

Julian's father, Ian, was also scholarly. After reading history at The
Queens' College, Oxford he narrowly missed gaining an academic
appointment and went instead to teach history at King Edward's
School, Birmingham (where he had, among his pupils, both Enoch
Powell and the distinguished theologian Christopher Evans). His
own father, an Oxford graduate, could also have been an academic,

---

1. See *Some Writings of Julian Harvey*, section 1, pp. 171–73.

but eschewed that career in favor of devoting his life to the ministry of a country parson in the High Anglican tradition. The headmaster of Ian's preparatory school had wanted to enter him for a scholarship at a top public school, but, for apparently sentimental reasons ("St. Augustine's old place"), Ian's father had insisted on the (at that time) relatively undistinguished King's School, Canterbury, where Ian contracted polio at the age of fourteen. This put an end to his sporting prowess (he had been a promising runner and cricketer) and also to the more serious ambitions he had for his life — he had hoped either to follow his father into the ordained ministry or to become a diplomat, but in those days both careers were closed to anyone as disabled as he was. His record as a schoolmaster was outstanding despite his unconventional methods: he tended to sit in the corner of the room and invite the boys who were interested to join him while the others did what they liked — in the end they all came to listen.

He moved from Birmingham in the 'thirties to teach history in the sixth form at Eton, but resigned early in the war over an issue to do with a boy who, he believed, had been unjustly expelled for performing a hoax. He was rescued from the entirely unsuitable employment he had found instead in Rugby by the father of one of his pupils, a senior civil servant at the Foreign Office, who brought him into the Research Department. When, after the war, this was merged into the general staff of the Foreign Office, Ian became eligible for a diplomatic post, and was awarded the prized appointment of consul in Florence in 1952, a post he held until he resigned a year after Jane's death in 1960. Thus, in the end, he fulfilled one of his original ambitions — and with great distinction (he was awarded the O.B.E. for his services). His other ambition — to become a priest — was also partially fulfilled before the end of his life, as we shall see later. But it was during his consular service that I first came to know him. His influence on me was profound.

And now here is Julian describing her own youth from very early days:

It is strange always to go back to the syringa tree! Raised a little by the mattress of my pram, so that I could see where she (my mother) would take me — down the grassy lawn. She would put me under the syringa tree, tidy and clean and gently wrapped, my thin safe "see-through" net, that hid nothing, being as white as a transparent cloud, but through which no bee or ant, no creatures could bother me. So there was nothing to stop me being able to watch each flower, their fragrance a joy to breathe. I was far too young to talk — it would have meant nothing (she knew, and I knew, peace!).

I did not know all she had to do those late evenings, struggling over her book reviews. Much time deeply involved with the Quakers, amazed at their accuracy and realization of all that was fearful, tragic or unjust in the world. She realized it (Edgbaston) was, and still is, a place to be.

I could watch the bees going from flower to flower, carrying the pollen in their neat pocket — food for their bee-fellows, and their succour. Fragrance everywhere. I loved it more and more. So much of them my father knew — words were no matter.

Then suddenly, and most oddly, I knew something from an earlier time, a distinctive scene. In the upstairs drawing room of a tiny place at the far end of a big garden. My parents had no house, for I had come into their world, sudden and unexpected, near Bournemouth, on an expedition to Shelley's home. Where could they live? He was to teach history at King Edward's (and very soon). Now that great teacher of Italian at Birmingham University, Linetta di Castelvecchio (dramatic, and always with her red wig and spats) said, "I have a small place — a stable in the days of horses and carriages (long before cars), and just at the end of my lovely garden. You will come?"

It is strange, for here I remember my mother clearly, her legs crossed in a sort of chair, holding me gently and safely on an angle of her right leg. I can see her bending a little to hold me while she chanted gently, "Ride a cock horse to Banbury Cross...."

How lovely that was, her voice clear as crystal, the rhythm of it unhurried, exciting, and she was the words and the music!

Is it odd that it returned to me so certainly? A small bare room above, the stable below, the two of us on this strange adventure! Sky, a tall tree, a bit of that big garden below....

I grew. Time went on. She did not believe too much in school for the very young, though she did believe in seeing, watching, and in movement and growing slowly. Much I learnt from Ian, my father, of butterflies and of growing things and, oh, that wild strawberry bed at the far end of the garden, to me a strange forest of perfect threefold leaves. He said, "If you sit on your small chair and are quite quiet and quite still you'll see a sudden movement of the leaves and you'll realize something — a special creature, perhaps, is there! And after a little, if you wait, you can very, very gently move those leaves apart." I did, and there was the Golden King looking at me with those wonderful dark eyes of his — the "Frog King" in his forest.

"Listening, seeing and movement too," my mother said. She had heard the Church of England school (a fine institution at the top of our hill) was having lessons in Greek dancing for girls rather older, in simple green frocks that let arms and legs have space for movement. They would allow me to join them, she was sure. They did, and she made me a pale, pale pink frock, simple, like theirs. In that great big room, in their green frocks — oh the peace and the delight — listening, seeing and movement now was all that mattered.

(My father was the same. He had won every race at his prep school, every cricket match, till polio got him; but no bitterness marred him. He learnt to watch, knew which song belonged to which bird. He was to teach the older would-be historians at Eton).

The garden, my syringa tree, my golden frog king were left for a dull house on a narrow street full of cars ceaselessly crossing over the bridge at Windsor. Too much to do — but my mother found, just across the road, a PNEU school, with fields beyond it. "They have good ideas," she said. I knew no one. Our first class was "Picture study." We were handed out not very large black and brown prints. These are by a famous artist, Peter de Hooch. Look at them very carefully. Then tell me what you see, or think." How I hated them. We would have them — and her — twice a week. Nature study was better, I being quick to find the caterpillars. The others did not seem interested.

It was "Back to Tables" now. "You must learn them by heart. It is essential, and necessary for life." Quietness followed (I had not done them ever!) "You," she said, "have not learnt one by heart. So take your desk. Go into the lower class." Humiliation crept over me as I stumbled there, aware of looks of scorn. I could not do it. I was back waiting for the leaves of the wild strawberries to move!

But the class in the gym of the great school had nothing to do with my school. My father would bravely come, among the nursemaids and the one very serious mother. And at the end of it he said, "When you are racing don't ever look behind you to see how the other one is getting on. Just go. Go as if you were going to the full moon. You get there then." I never forgot. Shame left me. And after that I won every running race in the PNEU at the end of each summer!

What could my mother do? She would try another school. This one: "modern, wise, caring surely?" But finding one child there was in hospital having run through the glass doors and another — much worse — from running, as allowed, for miles and then falling into a lime pit — "Useless for you," she said, "who's never stopped exploring."

Now it was Downe House, started by Olive Willis, an old Somervillean and, too, approved of by her beloved tutor. She made me a chic white coat, so that I looked intelligent. But it was my father that the head mistress fell for: he had just her understanding of children (and people). At once he was to be on her Governing Body. And, yes, they could just manage to take me.

Oh that first term! I went down from class to class, and waiting for a "Jane queue" (their horrid word for a loo), and inside trying to read my mother's letters. "Time and the Hour run through the roughest days" — hiding my tears. I'd disappear into the woods all around us, and then, very slowly, read the letter and bear the derision. In our large bedrooms there was always one divisive person. We had a different bedroom each term (agonizing to discover them on arriving!). But then, to my joy, I was in one small, sunny room with a clever, caring girl. Vividly I remember my grandfather sending me a copy of "Virginibus Puerisque." From it I would pick out a word and learn to spell it — nor have I ever forgotten "manufacture" — it was the first.

Was it the beginning, or (dare I say it) the rainbow at the end? The alone-walks made me realize this awful necessity. Gradually I improved. A term or two later I had overcome some things, even had a good report. So it was up to me, I knew, to brave Miss Heather, the formidable friend of the head mistress (a brilliant mathematician from Cambridge but I did not know that then). But she was the one who, like the "Waves," worked out each form. "I could go up," I said, "to so and so, and there work for my exams" (thinking there might be hope for a university). She looked at me. "Hm, you've done well. Yes I think you could, next term."

Different now, and easier. I was accepted. Old joys returned. Far away I found a deserted pool, tall trees round it — poetry itself — or week-end summer afternoons under the apple trees in the wild orchard, for discussion and thought. Up in our "seniors'" tower, with the woods below us and the small Grecian cupola with the roses below, we could carve a new sonnet to add to our predecessors' on those low wooden chairs left by an odd American order who had left them behind.

At nearly eighteen it was hard to leave Downe. We could discuss our work with many of the staff. And with Olive Willis, our head mistress — oh, those "Sunday teas" when she would describe visits of Charles Williams, his voice and manner, talking of Shakespeare, and so many things. "Yes," she said, "the walls would go out, we were in his world."

And then there was Oxford. Ian, my father, still deep in the

Research Department of the Foreign Office, would do some history with me. So it was Charlemagne he thought we would do. And vivid he made it! No fuss or hurry. It was exactly the same way that had enabled me to find my Golden Frog.

Exams at Oxford, in that icy winter, blackbirds stuck by ice to frozen branches. An old lady brought us hot water bottles that, though needed, stopped our thinking! Somehow I weathered it. Miss McKisick, my tutor, in my very first tutorial, said, "Miss McMaster, do you know the dates of the Kings and Queens of England?" And then, later on, the complications of justice in past times: "Miss Hennard (of LMH) has written on that — but put a wet towel round your head if you read her."

There were Societies, alive and calling, so I chose one, "Cosmos," full of tall, clever young men, but wise and caring much for the state of the world. Their successors got hold of endless dull ambassadors. I was sorry. Numbers dropped!

It was spring again. In Somerville gentle tennis went on, and under the tall trees were some "Colchicum," pale and magic and lovely. Yet I could not write a poem for them, my "ending gone," I said to myself. Then, suddenly, I was asked to be head of Cosmos. It could have great speakers, who knew and cared, with wisdom and experience for us all! It worked, and it grew. First it was Cardinal Mindszenty with Fr Corbishley (the Jesuit) and, with him, the great expert on Hungary. A quiet dinner with them, and then a full, expectant hall! It was exciting, and real.

It was soon after she left Oxford with a history degree that her father was posted to Florence. She went with her parents and helped them establish the extraordinarily welcoming and informal home by which a steady stream of visitors was surprised and enchanted. Here is a flavor of her life in those years, taken from her diary:

Sunday May 15th 1955 — in Florence
    It does not seem very like Sunday. Rain, steady and peaceful. The corn under the olive trees is long and very green. 'The

Duke of Gloucester must be in his aeroplane by now', we said over breakfast, looking down over the olive trees across the narrow Via San Leonardo.

We were to meet him at the Grand Hotel. 'Pretini' (Mr Lelli) arrived first. He was to meet General Alexander and the Duke, for he had been so brave in helping our soldiers, and later had been taken in chains through the streets of Florence. He was even tortured, but had shown no fear. Now came General Mannering — thin, tall, interesting, not unlike a French aristocrat (it was he who had such an incredible escape right across Italy, disguised as a half-mad Italian peasant). Next came General Alexander, a trifle grumpy (but then he was in charge).

The Duke was very silent. He stood as though some aura divorced him a little from everyone else; rather red in the face, yet redeemed by those blue eyes. What would the Italians make of him — tall, yes, but sombre? I was afraid that 'Pretini' was disappointed, and that saddened me.

Now Ian, my father, went ahead with the Duke. Jane and I followed with our rare chauffeur, who went ahead to the Uffizi, where we all got out at the same time. The main doors were open wide, and Professor Rossi was waiting. People waiting to get in were being kept back, but only for a little time. (During all the eight years we were there, and maybe before, on Sunday mornings the Uffizi was open and free for all. My mother would go there to draw a little, unable to resist the native Florentines who loved it so. I wondered, was it not some pull of hers that had achieved this special time for our visitors? For so many of the generals had said, "The Duke will not be interested in art.")

Here the Duke seemed even taller. And, moving with this slightly detached aura, people dropped back to let him pass. He and I walked together up the endless flights of stairs. It was very hot and breathless, but he went on indomitably, and would not rest.

"This is Cimabue's famous Madonna, 13th century," I said (it was one my mother loved because it was so like her beloved history tutor, Maud Clarke.) We seemed to have lost the others, and my voice seemed suddenly very thin, as though it were getting lost somewhere on the top of a very high mountain. Had the tall Duke heard me? I could not tell. He looked at it, and at the Simone Martini (which I loved) but I think the Cimabue meant more to him.... But now we were with Botticelli's "Spring." I told him about the Joust Giuliano di Medici had given for La Bella Simonetta Vespucci, and the Poliziano poem that had inspired the painting. I believe he liked it: he remained there, still and concentrated. Today Simonetta's face was extraordinarily beautiful, a strange, wistful, poignant sadness as though she knew she was passing. It stood out oddly as the central piece; and the Graces were "beautiful flowers" and the wood, life with all its complexity. How burdened she seemed, and how lovely.

But now we moved slowly to the great Van der Goes. Did the Duke like it? I don't know. "The children," I said, "are so beautifully painted, so still and listening. And — interesting to see an Italian family by a Dutch painter." "Yes, the children," he said, meditatively. But on to Leonardo — he was with my mother now, but I could see it all. He was deeply interested in the great Leonardo cartoon. He traced with his fingers round the swirl of faces and the horses' heads, and Leonardo rose up out of the Renaissance world to meet the present and to fight on with the future, just as though his fingers were on the springs of the world, all its weight and logic, mystery and boundless form. We passed the angel Leonardo had painted at fourteen, and so on to the Map Room with only the Annunciation. To me it brought an extraordinary peace that I'd not felt before, and also, I think, to the Duke.

Now, very slowly, we went back to the room where Uccello's "Battle Scene" is. "His great Battle Scene," I said. The Duke stood in front, Florentines making way for him. "Incredible," he said, "amazing," "incredible picture." " 'And the rider was a chessman," I said, adding, "and don't you like the way they are hunting happily while the battle is going on?"

And the Duke laughed, really laughed! "Yes," he said, with a burst and a shower of Hanoverian laughter. General Alexander appeared beside us. "Extraordinary the way they did not understand perspective," he said, rather crossly, "so simple, too." Now Rossi was beside us. He had asked me to present him to General Alexander. Now he followed us down the long steep stairs, holding a very beautiful reproduction of Van der Goes's great painting with its fine flowers in the foreground. I said he must give them to the Duke. Which he did, but the Duke thanked him rather inaudibly from his great height. So poor Rossi, not being tall, looked bothered, and so, worried for him, I said, "The Duke says he would love them" — quite forgetting I was talking in English and the Duke was just beside me!

But now the generals were fussing, and Hawling and Alexander looked intensely at their watches. The cars were waiting at the steps of the Palazzo Vecchio. "The Duke wishes to say good-bye to you," someone — probably Mannering — said. The Duke had a very beautiful smile, oddly unlike the rest of his rather immobile face. It crinkled and showered like sun on a very blue sea. And the others — meaning Generals Mannering and Alexander and Crocker (with an amazingly kindly, elderly face) and Hawling (vivid, with some green, quicksilver, leprechaun quality).... I was sorry he was going. A feeling of speed in him and of intellect I had not met for so long, if ever — magnificent. (P.S. From the Grand Hotel I drove home. Ian, my father, had gone with them to call at Montegufoni (on their way to Pistoia). He said "it was the perfect finish." Osbert [Sitwell] was waiting on the steps, and walked up with the Duke. Edith standing in all her finery, looking magnificent. The Duke and she got on wonderfully.)

Such was Julian's life in the early fifties, living with her parents in Florence (a remarkably close and trusting trio), attending formal functions, and social events, entertaining an endless stream of visitors of every kind and class — official guests, Florentine notables, English visitors, but also a number of retired English governesses who had spent years in large Florentine households and been left with so little to live on that they would have to be coaxed to accept any hospitality since they could not afford the bunch of flowers which (until they met Jane McMaster) they believed were *de rigueur* for any social call. And in that society Julian shone as a bright star, with her knowledge of history and art, her literary inspirations, her charm and graciousness, and her exceptional beauty. When she left Oxford her history tutor wrote of her, "She seemed to have a most original mind, to be able to think and to have an exceptional intelligence. ... She has insight and imagination. Now that she has become more mature I should expect her to be capable of distinguishing herself. ... "Distinguished" she certainly became during those years in Florence.

But it was there that Julian also developed another talent, which had been in her since childhood in a rudimentary form, but was now suddenly brought to full growth — painting. Flowers were her favorite subject, and she had a gift of giving them life and vitality on the canvas; but in Florence she took the opportunity of attending life classes and in due course could do portraits and landscapes with equal facility. One of these — a view from their villa in a storm — won an award from a local art society, and an early oil painting of tulips in a vase won the approbation of Annigoni, who lived nearby, became a friend, and did a pastel portrait of Julian (which unfortunately never pleased the family since it was in his characteristic monumental style — the very opposite of Julian's character!). Julian always insisted that she was a beginner and an amateur, even after she had sold a number of pictures in London and had two very successful exhibitions. For her, painting was rather an expression of something deeply felt which she had a deep urge to turn into art. While still in Florence she wrote this in her diary:

> I painted the Madonna Lilies. I can never really paint — it is only a line here or a shape there that occasionally captures a flame. And in doing it there comes the most extraordinary feeling of mental rest — more real than any sleep. It brings a directness: only the lily and you, a communion where there can

be no fear … the kind of communion so rare with persons. If it were not for this I would not feel justified in doing it.

It was a similar impulse that also led her to write poetry from a very early age. When I first read some of her poems, I was brutally critical (and my insensitivity caused Julian much anguish: she had gone through agonies before resolving to show them to me). They seemed to be in such a private language, so innocent of awareness of poetical cliché, so allusive within the context of very personal experiences, that I doubted their appeal outside the circle of her friends and family. But I was wrong. She had already had one or two poems published in poetry journals, and later, throughout our time in Oxford, she belonged to a group of poets who regularly published a yearbook of their work. Here are some lines from her verses about Fr. Greg Wilkins, a Kelham monk who came to do duty one summer at the Anglican church in Florence, shocking some of the regular congregation by his informality and directness but attracting some younger people to join the congregation. Julian formed a close friendship with him and they had long walks together around Florence:

> Greg Wilkins was like a ship's mast!
> He did not notice the wind's blast;
> Rather he seemed to enjoy
> Being devoid of anything
> That might in some way fret or cloy
> The odd uninhibited fling
> That spiritual nakedness gave
> Him in such a sensuous way.
> He wore sandals in the nave.…
> I'd not seen a face so relaxed,
> A kind of shorn or born-again
> Look, but his spade-filled phrases taxed
> The congregation and gave pain
> To the Misses Good and Pringle,
> Who did not like their roseate world
> Miraged away to nothingness

Or the gossip-tapestry furled....
A sort of desperate unease
Clutched at their throats and prevented
Them speaking — as of some disease
They dared not mention; tormenting them.
They talked of hats. But when, next year,
They did not any longer see
Him, holes had begun to appear
In the gossip-tapestry.

CHAPTER 3

Commitment: Marriage and Ordination

S uch was the person — painter, poet, and social luminary — whom I had fallen in love with under circumstances that seemed, at the time and in retrospect, either providentially or diabolically contrived to take me captive. And I was indeed captivated — by her beauty, by her brilliantly allusive conversation, her artistic sensibility, her scintillating letters, her spontaneity, and her charm. When I returned to Munich there was no doubt I was deeply affected, and we were writing letters to each other several times a week. One of the first I wrote to her was from Berlin. My time in Munich was coming to an end, but I was determined to visit Berlin before I left Germany and set aside a week before my return to do so. In the letter, sandwiched between paragraphs of emotional excitement and introspection, was this description of my visit to a city of which the life was being sustained only by the AirLift from the West.

> Berlin is extraordinary.... The immediate impact was of a deadly *quiet* city. Practically no traffic, (for where would cars come from in a city under siege?), not very many people. The second impact goes closely with the first — huge empty spaces, wide streets linking only a few buildings together, immense vistas. Berlin must always have been somewhat diffuse. Like London (and there are many similarities with London) there is not one centre, but several, separated by great distances (for Berlin is gigantic). Even these centres were not compact,

but built with grandiose expansiveness; and now that acres of buildings have been destroyed, the distances seem even greater, the open spaces predominate. The loose conjunction of isolated buildings, the silence, the lack of people, contribute to a sense of abandon that is almost apocalyptic.

And yet there is another side to it. Berlin is luxurious. Superb shops, fine hotels, smooth cafés, several theatres, smart restaurants, night clubs and so forth. The Berliners themselves are well dressed, the whole atmosphere is one of sophistication — a capital city. Of course, the contrast is not accidental. The effort to reinstate a real capital in the middle of the Soviet zone was deliberate and intense. The difference between the drab empty streets of the East sector and the fashionable blaze of a famous spot in the West like the Kurfürstendamm has been made as sharp as possible. Where everything, from bottles of milk to motor cars, has to be imported, under difficult conditions, from West Germany, the sense of plenty is astounding. The new buildings which have gone up from the rubble heaps are confident and handsome, without a trace of emergency or forced economy (admittedly the Americans have paid for many of them). The food is infinitely better than in Munich, the cafés crowded. West Berlin asserts itself with a vigorous display of civilized, sophisticated living. But of course this is concentrated in a very small area, a few notable streets. There are not enough people, enough buildings, enough transport, for it to be able to cover more than a fraction of the city area. One only has to walk a minute or two away from the neon lights to be once again in the rubble, the silence, and the desolate perspectives.

The people are of course highly self-conscious: they are vividly aware of the curious role they are playing. Heroism is perhaps too strong a word — one cannot be heroic for ten years. But the atmosphere is rather like that of London during the air raids: there is a kind of conspiratorial friendliness in every look, a continual recurrence in every conversation to the conditions of living. The strangeness, sinisterness, of these conditions cannot be exaggerated. Russian and East German policemen stand on every street at the sector frontier, the city has two currencies, two governments, two faces. In the east it is all darkness and slogans, with even less traffic than in the West; and the final glory of Unter den Linden, the palace which formed one end of that superb street, is now a large square with a tribune, a setting for communist manifestations. Everything is precarious: tomorrow it may be impossible to cross the frontier at all, today your brief-case may be searched when you do. Even from the West, there is for most Berliners no escape. They must just go on living in their little bastion, the state of siege continues inexorably. The situation is grotesque, and at the same time deadly serious. Berlin (if I may risk the oxymoron) is the burning point of the Cold War.

I am deeply grateful that I came, first because Berliners are so different from Munichers that I can hardly believe myself in the same country, secondly because the experience of the iron curtain is extraordinary and troubling....

In those days requirements for post-graduate work were extremely informal, and by the end of my time in Munich all I had to show for my research was one complete and one half-finished article for an academic journal. But one of these was recognized as well up to standard — anything but amateur. It became standard reading for specialists and students in the field, and I was tipped to become a top professor of Greek, though I had my own doubts about the capacity of my memory to carry sufficient freight of ancient texts in the long term. But apart from doubts about memory, which I sensed would always lend a touch of the amateur to my academic work, I had already begun to waver about following a university career. Was it not a way of insulating oneself from the real problems and difficulties of ordinary life? Had I not got some kind of leaning towards working with individual people rather than with books? I was to learn later that the life of a university teacher may be as committed to meeting individual needs and public policy issues as that of any other profession; but at this stage there were stirrings in me of a sense of vocation (as I took it to be) that led me, during one of my visits home, to give myself more time to decide between careers by applying for a post in the Talks Department in the BBC. I got a favorable response and was interviewed. But after I returned to Munich I heard nothing more, and when an offer of a lectureship in classics arrived from a London university college there seemed no good reason to refuse. However before accepting I thought it worth writing briefly to the BBC asking if they were still interested. I received a reply by telegram — "Situation open to you" — and accepted at once. Both I and my employers (who were amazingly generous and understanding) knew that this might be short term and temporary, since I was thinking increasingly seriously about being ordained.

At the BBC, the Talks Department was run in what seems to me now a remarkably enlightened way. At the beginning of each week the producers sat round a long table with the controller of the relevant program in the chair (I worked mainly for the Third, far the easiest to provide for with its tolerant and sophisticated audience: producing talks on the Home Service was a far more difficult and responsible task, and the Light Programme was a field for the real geniuses who could present serious material without the listener turning off the radio). At this meeting each of us was expected to come forward with proposals for talks or series of talks (always limited to eighteen and a half minutes). As soon as we had done so our colleagues would lay savagely into us, listing every possible objection and casting doubt on the worthiness of the idea. If one could defend oneself robustly and make a good enough case the controller would nod in agreement, saying, "All right, Mr. Harvey, go ahead." From that moment until the actual broadcast one was trusted to go one's own way with very little control or supervision. Only if the result was a disaster would some discipline be exerted.

In this liberal environment I learned the craft of nurturing and editing other people's work, which became one of my strengths later on. On one occasion I even had to write the script for a psychoanalyst who was asked to contribute to a series of talks on Freud for the Home Service. These had been planned through the usual BBC procedure of offering a heady lunch to a selected group of contributors in an inner cavern of Broadcasting House, in the expectation that a coherent scheme would emerge. The opposite happened on this occasion, and by the end the psychoanalysts were arguing fiercely among themselves without any apparent agreement about what the series should contain. I was then given the task of salvaging something from the wreckage, which I could do only by abandoning all further consultation and dealing with each of the contributors on their own. One of them turned out to be quite incapable of putting his thoughts together coherently, and after several attempts to help him I finally gave up and walked through some of the offices in the corridor looking for a secretary who had not much to do. Having found one, I dictated to her what I thought my psychoanalyst was trying to say and sent him the result, suggesting he used it as the basis of his talk. To my astonishment he accepted my script without question or alteration and delivered it verbatim as if it was his own.

On another occasion I had the privilege of editing and producing a talk by Yigael Yadin. He was in London on an official visit from Israel as military chief of staff. But he was also a leading archaeologist, and he found time to present the findings of his recent excavations at Hazor (allegedly one of Solomon's fortified cities) in a talk on the Third Programme. His English was fluent but not entirely correct, and I needed to make some alterations to his script. When we went through it together, I was amazed by the sharpness and subtlety of his mind, which instantly detected any nuance that did not exactly convey what he wanted to say. This archaeologist-turned-military-strategist impressed me deeply: he was surely a modern Renaissance man of prodigiously varied gifts and abilities. By coincidence, some ten years later, I was a lecturer on a Swan's Hellenic Cruise and had to introduce the passengers to the site, the tel, where the excavations had taken place. We were to be met by Yadin himself, who would take us around the site. But Swan's had not noticed that our arrival coincided with Israel's Independence Day, and that Yadin, the Chief of Staff, would be otherwise engaged. So I was asked to do it instead. I could remember the main points of Yadin's talk, but I knew that a few seasons' rain would have made the site unrecognizable. By good fortune I met a taxi driver who had been on the dig himself and remembered where the excavations had been. We dashed on ahead of the passengers and he led me on a lightning tour, pointing out the relevant features and getting round just as the earnest crowd of cruise passengers was approaching. Thanks to him, to my memories of Yadin's talk and a measure of bluff, I was able to convince them that they were being reliably shown around an otherwise unintelligible archaeological site. It was the gifted amateur in action.

In the course of the year the BBC actually offered me promotion; but by then I had made my decision to be ordained and secured a place for the following autumn at a theological college. I find it difficult to say when I first felt "called" to the priesthood. I remember I was a pious little boy, singing hymns in my bedroom and imagining myself preaching fiery sermons to convert the boys I saw being rough to each other in the village. I enjoyed the parish church services to which we always went on a Sunday and where I often played the organ — my father, an unbelieving agnostic, was firmly committed to "supporting the church" by his presence: he generally read the Lessons, greatly appreciating the prose of the King James Version. At school I conformed willingly to the regular chapel routine, and did the same at Oxford — at the time chapel attendance in my college was compulsory, and one's name was ticked by the college porter at the door: one had to make one's case to the provost if one wished not to go. But this was more a habit than a sign of conviction. I had met a young English evangelical in Brussels, who tried to convince me of my inherent sinfulness and my need for the saving work of Christ. This troubled me deeply for some time, and in reaction I distanced myself from anything religious other than church services, where I continued to feel somehow at home.

By the time I went to Munich, where there was no familiar place of worship, I was frankly unbelieving; but I continued to read Christian literature and my old sense of somehow belonging within the tradition of the Church of England never disappeared. On my visits home I sought out one or two wise priests who helped me to bring this instinctive loyalty into relation with the essence of the Christian religion, and my sense of being drawn to the priesthood seemed consonant with my urge to do something practical and pastoral alongside my academic ambitions. I doubt whether there was ever a moment when I could have said that I had experienced a "call"; but the project of ordination gradually became the one that seemed most to make sense of the shape of my life so far, despite my doubts about my fitness to be a priest, which continued to surface right up to the moment the bishop laid hands on me.

My decision to be ordained was accepted without opposition but without enthusiasm by my family. My mother who, being Anglo-Irish, had an utter contempt for all clergy, would have been horrified; but by this time she had died of cancer at the early age of fifty-three. She had been ill for many months, and my time in Munich had been broken into by several long visits home to keep her company when my father, still practicing as a barrister, had to be away from home. I suppose I must never have felt very close to her, since I have singularly few vivid recollections of her. It is possible too that the long periods that she perforce had to abandon me to the care of others in Switzerland had caused some rift in our relationship, though I have no conscious recollection of it. Nevertheless I do recall being devastated by her death and being unable to cope with my father's excessively British restraint in the face of it. Indeed, behind the mask, I soon found he was very deeply affected, and indeed, to my sadness, embittered: on top of my sister's disablement, which put an end both to her career with horses and to any realistic prospect of marriage, this second blow seemed to him to be one injustice too many. As for my decision to be ordained, he made no objection. He was a redoubtable agnostic — he had one of the most brilliant minds I have ever known — and had attempted to dissuade me from being confirmed along with my contemporaries at school by making me read chunks of Gibbon and Bernard Shaw (the attempt, of course, was counter-productive, and I went ahead with my confirmation in the school chapel). But he now accepted my decision simply on the pragmatic grounds that I would probably do less harm than good as a clergyman.

During my time at the BBC Julian was still living with her parents in the glittering world of Florence, making only occasional visits to England to attend to their house in Oxford and to pay brief visits to me in London and in our family home in Buckinghamshire, where my father and sister gave her as warm a welcome as could be expected from rather conventional people who found Julian as unexpected and elusive as I had done. Indeed her warmest welcome came from May, a simple but wise and caring country woman from the village who was our devoted housekeeper for many years. She had seen me growing up from early boyhood and evidently sensed that I would get from Julian the affection of which she thought (perhaps correctly) I had been somewhat deprived by my parents. In London we did the rounds of conventional courtship — opera, ballet, oysters for lunch at Wheeler's, dinners in Soho (which were often quite fraught: Julian had been firmly taught by her mother never to leave food on her plate, but any nervousness in the company of others prevented her from eating, and if there was some tension between us at the time the resulting impasse meant we might still be at the table when the waiters were trying to close for the night). And of course we discussed and wrote at length to each other about my decision to be ordained, which she reluctantly accepted, though with some anxiety lest the somewhat monastic training (as it was in those days) might reinforce my puritanical and secretive tendencies.

Thus we were both still uncertain about whether we should get married when, in September 1956, I began a two-year course of theological training at Westcott House in Cambridge. This was regarded as a liberal college in the Church of England, giving its students opportunities for attending university lectures as well as providing the necessary pastoral training. It was presided over by a principal, Ken Carey, who had no academic pretensions but had inherited from the principal of his own student time, B. K. Cunningham, a distinctive style of deeply pastoral and sensitive oversight. I shared with most of the students an unreserved admiration and affection for him, and listened intensely to his devotional admonitions in the chapel. It was only a few years later, in the turmoil of the sixties, that his unashamedly patriarchal style came into question and the somewhat obsequious ethos of the college began to disintegrate. It was then that he left to become Bishop of Edinburgh, where he deeply missed the society of the young men he had been caring for during many years (he had a homosexual tendency which only then became a subject for comment) and had, perhaps, a less successful ministry there. But his friendship remained constant, and he labored valiantly to help me adjust to the new persona I had framed for myself, that of future priest and pastor.

Adjustment certainly was not easy. I was ready to accept my unpreparedness for ordination in terms of spiritual development and pastoral experience, and applied myself zealously to learning about the practice of prayer, the conduct of services, the demands of pastoral situations and the vicissitudes of personal faith, which indeed I underwent in full measure, with long periods of uncertainty over whether I should proceed at all. But when it was a matter of intellectual formation and academic theological study I had to cope with a major obstacle — my own (and even others') opinion of myself as an already qualified scholar. I could not think of myself as a student again — I even went on dressing, rather absurdly, in a suit rather than informally as a student, I perversely preferred to read some of the standard theological books in the original German rather than in translation, and I was secretive about my own rather indifferent progress in my theological studies. There was an option to take a university degree in theology, which would have been the obvious course for a budding academic to take before ordination. Instead I took the much less rigorous course offered by the church authorities, with very mediocre results.

Partly, I think, the reasons were intellectual. Trained in linguistic precision by my classical studies, and having done all my philosophy according to the analytical school then regnant in Oxford — and so developing an instinctive mistrust of any propositions that sounded metaphysical — it was only when working on the Greek text of the New Testament that I felt at home (my Hebrew never reached a serviceable level for doing the same with the Old Testament). And dogmatic theology, with its tendency toward abstract and unverifiable propositions, held no attraction for me at all — or rather, I simply could not get my mind around it. But in part, also, my renunciation (as I thought) of an academic career made me feel too detached from serious study of another subject to take it very seriously; I was becoming more interested in the practical elements of preparing to be a pastor and in wrestling with the spiritual doubts and crises that are part of an ordinand's experience. Whatever the reasons, I emerged from the expert and generous tutelage of Westcott House, ready (I hoped) for ordination, but without any further academic qualification and (crucially) with only a superficial knowledge of great areas of the standard theological curriculum. The result was that for the whole of the twenty years that I subsequently found myself in university employment I had no degree in the subject I was teaching — an anomaly that was still possible, and by no means unique, in the Oxford of those days, and which I rectified only when I had finally left Oxford by taking a Doctorate of Divinity on the strength of the books I had written.

By the spring of 1957 Julian and I felt sufficiently sure about ourselves and each other to announce our engagement. Then followed a spell of fraught negotiations about the wedding, conducted in a stream of letters — sometimes even telegrams — that passed between Florence and Cambridge. There was first the question of where it should be — Florence or England. Julian had formed close friendships and attracted many admirers during her years in Florence, and there was much charm in the idea of a celebration in the gorgeously decorated and furnished Palazzo her parents were living in. But all my instincts were against it — the obstacle it would present to my family and closest friends, the musical and liturgical limitations of the Anglican church in Florence, and perhaps also a touch of my puritanical distaste for anything that suggested ostentation or extravagance (though the unconventional and easily accessible lifestyle of Julian's parents hardly merited any such suspicion). In the end we compromised by agreeing on the University Church in Oxford as common ground for us all (we were both Oxford graduates, as were three of our four parents). For a service there I was able to call on a distinguished cathedral organist whom I had known earlier and who gathered a choir and used music gleaned from a little-known manuscript that was an early setting of the Prayer Book words. But for some time I had to get used to the McMaster tendency to go back over even this decision as if it had never been made.

There was still much uncertainty over the details of the service: should it be a Eucharist, satisfying my leanings as a future priest but perhaps causing discomfort and embarrassment to some of our guests? How much music, how much preaching, how much of the full Prayer Book service? Even the choice of hymns created tensions. Julian wanted "Jerusalem," I protested that social reform was not on the agenda, and alternative lists went back and forth. In the end Ken Carey, who was to take the service, took advantage of a visit of Julian's to Cambridge to talk it through with us, and firm decisions were eventually made. But the process was a foretaste of the clash between our inherited cultures: on Julian's side there was an instinctive impatience with rules set by convention, on mine an intransigence over details of which I was too immature to see the insignificance. The invitations were beautifully printed in Florence, and Julian brought them to me with justifiable pride. But my Christian name with an "h" was of course unknown to an Italian printer, and I appeared on the card as *Antony Harvey*. Outraged, I had them printed again (much less elegantly) in England. I may have been justified: my family and their friends would have been surprised and even shocked by the misspelling. But I was still quite insensitive to the hurt that could be caused by my summary rejection of something in which my future in-laws had evidently taken pride.

By the time we finally got married I was half way through my course in Cambridge, and after a honeymoon that took us by slow stages to Corfu — I won't say "easy stages," because there was much discomfort and some alarms on the way, such as the evident danger of Julian being taken off my hands and out of my protection by the burly Yugoslav captain of the tiny ship in which we were slowly progressing down the Adriatic — we started our married life in the top floor flat of a private house in Madingley Road. Neither of us was young enough to want to put off having a family, and our first child announced her conception quite early on. The result was that Julian felt unwell for much of the time, and in addition the theological college regime imposed very strict limitations on the time we could spend together. Apart from Saturday evenings I was expected to be in college every day from early morning until often quite late in the evening, and Julian's own appearances there were limited to the early service and breakfast on Sundays. As she confronted her loneliness and shivered in the unfamiliar damp of the Cambridgeshire climate she could hardly have been expected not to feel regret for the sunshine and charm of the Florentine surroundings that she had exchanged for partnership with a man trying to discipline himself in preparation for the austere life (as he then imagined it) of a priest.

Yet there were compensations. Julian already had some acquaintances in Cambridge and naturally expected they would provide a welcome contrast to the stern environment of Westcott House. In the event it turned out differently: little by little she became a valued outside member of the college community, and before we left she had written a short play that was performed in the college under the direction of a student who had been a professional actor — the usual exclusion rules were waived so that she could be present at all the rehearsals. There was also the society of other ordinands' wives, in particular the wife and family of a former naval commander: they were already friends by the time we got married and their son was a page at our wedding. By the end, Julian had found her contacts with the college, even under the restrictions imposed by the regime, far more enjoyable than anything offered by the social contacts she already had with the university. Yet there was a dark shadow over this first year of our marriage. Julian's mother had been diagnosed with cancer soon after she returned to Florence following our wedding and she was being nursed in the home of a religious order. After some months it was decided to bring her back to a nursing home in Oxford. There she spent the last months of her life. Ian, of course, had to remain in Florence to fulfill his consular duties, and Julian and I took on the responsibility of family care as best we could. This was in the later months of Julian's pregnancy and my own final examinations and preparations before ordination, and our visits to Oxford were necessarily sporadic.

One crisis in particular remains in my memory. It concerns Jane's religion, which had always been implicit rather than explicit: she attached little importance to rites and ceremonies (though she would always go to church when she could) compared with living true to her fundamental Christian convictions. Accordingly, when the Cowley Fathers, in their High Church tradition, were invited to attend to her spiritual needs in the nursing home, a conflict arose. Seeing that she was terminally ill, the Father insisted she should make her confession and arranged to come again the following week to hear it. This had never been Jane's practice, and caused her considerable dismay and anxiety. When I heard of this, I consulted Ken Carey, our principal — whose training included instruction in hearing confessions but also the proviso that this practice should never be insisted upon — and he virtually commanded me to get in the car and drive straight over to Oxford to countermand the threatened visit. For me, it was an early experience of the dangers of religious dogmatism, but also a valuable pointer to the nature of Julian's inner life. She, like her mother, attached little importance to the externals of religion — I doubt whether she could ever recite the Lord's Prayer correctly; her faith expressed itself at a much deeper level, indeed one of her advisers called her "a natural mystic." She read widely in the literature of prayer and spirituality, and felt completely at home with monks and nuns, of whom many became close friends and confidants — even the rift with the Cowley Fathers was soon healed to allow personal friendship with several of them to flourish. In my preparation for and early years of priestly discipline, regulated by times and seasons, rules and conventions, I was being slowly brought to find the heart of the matter elsewhere.

Jane died ten days before the birth of our first child. Ian's own faith, like Jane's, was unostentatious but profound. For the funeral he dressed in white, and insisted that the service should proclaim victory over suffering as much as grief over an early death (Jane was only 58 when she died). In the graveyard Julian, dressed in what we called her scarlet "Robin Hood" cloak, which we had bought together a few months previously, could be seen darting about among the mourners, insisting that they came back with us to the McMaster house in Park Town for refreshment. "There is the spirit of her mother," Ian whispered to me — and indeed the instinct to offer hospitality had always ruled the McMaster household. Where it derived from is a mystery: Ian's clerical father had been a punctilious widower, never allowing the routine of the household (presided over by two spinster sisters) to be disturbed by unexpected socializing, Jane's mother, who lived in a small village cottage and had herself been a widow for forty years already, had never been known to offer a meal to anyone. But the instinct was deep in Julian; and this was another of the benign influences which were gradually to release me from the restrictive formality of my upbringing.

Jane's legacy persisted in another and more surprising way. Our daughter Marina was born only a few days after her grandmother's death, and in her early years the continuity seemed quite uncanny. She excelled in exactly the same gifts: she could draw, she could sew, she could do anything with her hands, and she had the humor and the gift with strangers that had been so conspicuous in Jane. She even talked as if she had known her intimately. There was never any doubt that we were right to christen her Jane. But this had to be her second name: her first was a necessary gesture of appreciation to a godmother. Princess Marina had got to know Jane and Ian in Florence and become a close friend. When she heard of Jane's death and her granddaughter's birth following so soon after, she wrote at once to say that the two souls must have met on their way between heaven and earth — a pleasing fantasy which seemed nevertheless to be proved true by the strange familiarity which the child showed with her dead grandmother. And in fact her name turned out to be perfectly fitting. As soon as she could swim, Marina became dedicated to everything to do with the sea, from exploring the seabed in a diving suit to studying aquaculture and fisheries for her second degree. Princess Marina was a well-loved member of the royal family, and at the time hers was a popular Christian name; but in our daughter's case there was no option: it was chosen for us.

Her birth had been long drawn out and painful, and ended with a surgical delivery in the hospital. Added to the strain of Jane's last months and our own preparations for a move to my curacy in London (quite apart from the deeper tensions and anxieties involved in my coming ordination in September), I found myself physically exhausted and succumbed to a virulent strain of 'flu, which left me debilitated right through the period when we were moving house and preparing for a new way of life. Somehow Julian found the stamina to take on most of what I should have been doing to help her in addition to nursing the baby, while even during the residential retreat leading to ordination in St. Paul's Cathedral I was spending most of the time in bed, emerging only for meals and devotional addresses. Immediately afterwards my vicar, with great good sense, forbade me to begin work and advised us to leave our belongings in packing cases in our new house and go away for a spell by the sea until I recovered. We were offered hospitality in a guest house in Cornwall, where the landlady allowed us to leave the baby in her pram in the garden during the mornings. There she was perfectly happy, kicking and gurgling, until we came home from our walk along the cliffs, which I gradually became fit enough to extend from a few hundred yards to a few miles. The baby Marina cooperated astonishingly by demanding no attention all morning, and by the end of October I was able to return to London in good health.

The parish had no house for us, but with my father's help we had secured a lease on one not far from the church in Chelsea. It had a spacious ground floor room, which, after accommodating my mother's grand piano, still had room for entertaining parishioners, and three other stories with two small rooms each. At first we had far too little furniture for it, and were literally using packing cases for chairs; but the cheaper end of the King's Road had affordable second hand shops which helped us to meet basic needs. Then came the avalanche. My father-in-law was retiring from Florence, and we received a message from the Foreign Office that two crates of his belongings would be delivered to our house. Did we have a garage where they could be placed? Indeed we did not, and the crates remained on the pavement, blocking out the light from our front window (and greatly inconveniencing passers by), until we were able to stow the contents indoors. From that moment, until late in our married life, we were perpetually over-furnished and seriously encumbered with family possessions, a situation exacerbated when the McMaster house in Oxford was sold and its contents transferred to ours. This was yet another contrast with the principles of my upbringing, when I had always had my possessions in good order without any superfluity. With marriage I found myself for the first time living with a perpetually unfinished agenda to bring some order into the confusion of our belongings.

At that date (1958) the parish in Chelsea, outwardly so upper-class and respectable, was a rare social mix. The churchwardens were a distinguished civil servant and a retired shopkeeper, the housing was still partly requisitioned, well-off families living next door to identical-looking houses with a crowded family living on each floor. The Peabody Buildings down the road still had gaslight and a single tap and sink on each landing. The congregation ranged from well-known West End actors and actresses to Welsh tradesmen and the butler of a duchess; the resident verger (one of our best friends) was a gloriously authentic cockney. The vicar (François Piachaud) of this relatively small parish, south of the King's Road, was allotted two curates so that he could look after post-ordination training for the diocese. François was an exceptionally well-read and intellectually inquiring priest. Books were crammed into every floor of his tall Victorian vicarage, and he preferred talking about history or philosophy to discussing parochial problems; indeed his curates were constantly frustrated by his reluctance to allow us any regular staff meetings. Not that he left us without guidance, indeed this was his enduring gift to us: on any pastoral problem he brought to bear a rare combination of understanding, humor, and common sense, backed up by a liberal theology that at the time could be called Modernist (he was a committed member of the Modern Churchmen's Union). When, as a young curate, I was in despair over one female parishioner who periodically presented me with larger-than-life personal and spiritual problems — "What on earth can I say to her?" I asked — he saved me with his eminently sensible advice, delivered with a chuckle, "Just give her heart!" His unshakable belief in my abilities, combined with his gentle molding of my pastoral efforts, were an influence on me for good that I look back to with gratitude. He was still in the same post and the same house when I came to Westminster Abbey twenty years later, and our friendship never wavered.

During the four years of my curacy (during which two more daughters were born to us) I persevered as best I could with some academic study, working my way through some thick German commentaries on the Bible and translating a small German theological book for the SCM Press. But my real interests were more practical. I created a booth to launch Christian Aid Week (an innovation fifty years ago) on a pavement in the King's Road and persuaded a bishop and other church and civic dignitaries to man it. I organized two charity balls in the town hall with Tommy Kinsman and his band. In those days a band leader took control of the whole evening and gave it a shape and adjusted the mood according to his instincts for a successful evening — Kinsman was an acknowledged master of the art. I also visited tirelessly, making friends both among the poorest and among the well off, spending many probably fruitless hours with an alcoholic house painter and finding a refreshing welcome from the likes of Agatha Christie and Sybil Thorndike (though also a painful rebuff from another well-known writer). One of the most rewarding ventures was the creation of a small discussion group among the young professionals, mainly lawyers and doctors, who lived in Chelsea. They were of our own age, and became close friends of Julian and myself. They gave me the chance to sharpen my own capacity for debate and to probe my own faith, and their friendship lasted long after we left Chelsea.

Before leaving Chelsea there were some opportunities for travel. Being by now fairly fluent in both French and German, I was taken on to do some simultaneous translating at international meetings by what was then the British Council of Churches. In 1960 there was a meeting of the Council of European Churches in unusual circumstances. It was to have been in Denmark; but it transpired that this would exclude the representatives from East Germany, who at that time would not have been able to obtain visas for a NATO country. However the Danish government minister for religious affairs was unwilling to lose the kudos of hosting the meeting, and commissioned a Danish ship on which we were all accommodated. We then sailed out in the Baltic until we came near enough to the Swedish coast for the East German delegates (who had easily obtained visas for Sweden) to come in a small boat to join us.

I remember vividly the emotion when this brave party arrived in a dinghy, were hoisted aboard and greeted with long embraces by their fellow Germans from the West from whom they had been separated since the frontier between East and West Germany had been closed in 1956. Even more moving was the moment when, at the end of the conference, we did the same in reverse and saw the small boat with the East Germans bobbing away in the dusk towards the Swedish coast, none knowing when, if at all, they would be able to see their friends again. The official languages for such meetings were English, French, and German; and since all the talk was about church and theology (my own subjects) I had no difficulty with the vocabulary, and found the technique of listening to a speech through earphones and reproducing it in English as it went along quite easy to learn — though we interpreters did sometimes have difficulty keeping up when a long German sentence kept us waiting until it reached the verb at the end!

Not long afterwards I was invited to do the same at the World Council of Churches Assembly in New Delhi. This was indeed an adventure. We were housed in Western-style hotels, but economically — that is to say, with four beds in rooms which would have been small for two; and our evening meals had simple Indian menus which we were obligingly helped to choose from by the assiduous young waiters. Most of us had some stomach troubles as a result, but none were seriously incapacitated. The Assembly itself took place in a big conference center, which was well equipped with booths for the translators in all the meeting rooms, and this large gathering of church people from all over the world attracted much interest from the local press. At that time the WCC was dominated by Americans, whose life-style was in even sharper contrast with that of India than our own. As we emerged from the sessions on to the steps outside the building they did not hesitate to light up cigarettes and cigars. Their appearance, and doubtless ours also, gave a certain bizarre piquancy to a headline I saw in the paper next day: MEN OF GOD GATHER IN DELHI.

I have an uncomfortable recollection that I did not behave at all well at the beginning. I had travelled out in eager expectation of using my recently acquired skill in simultaneous interpreting. When I arrived, one of the conference staff calmly directed me to the office where other translators were assigned to rendering existing texts of German speeches into English. Affronted, I rebelled, and, despite causing some bad feeling, was eventually granted the job I wanted. In retrospect I cannot feel proud of a conceit that made me think myself superior to the mere translators; and I have an uneasy feeling that I did something of the same kind on the previous conference in the Baltic. Perhaps more serious was the unease we all felt at being housed, fed and transported in a style so different from that which was possible for any but the most wealthy Indians. But I had a chance to make up for this when, the conference over, there were a few days free for sightseeing, and I was invited to stay with the priests of the Cambridge Brotherhood in the heart of Old Delhi. Not merely did they live with an austere simplicity which brought them much closer to the realities of Indian life, but their cool, simple house was in a populous part of the city, so that I could get a feel of the country there far more than as a tourist visiting the Taj Mahal — which of course I also did. My one regret was that Julian could not come with me: her artist's eye would have been excited by so much of what was around me, and visiting India had always been one of her long-term ambitions. But she was at home looking after our second baby, and anyway, in those days spouses were strictly not invited!

Then, just before we left London, there was the United States, and this time our third baby could be weaned in time for Julian to leave her and the other children with a trusted nanny and accompany me. The occasion was an ecumenical preaching tour organized, again, by the British Council of Churches. The strategy here was to take advantage of the fact that August was the time when American clergy (like anyone else) preferred to go "on vacation," and their churches were happy to pay fees for a Sunday replacement which were sufficient to defray our travelling and subsistence costs until the following Sunday. We did a different church each week, and were entertained by lay members of each congregation in their houses. I had done my best to prepare myself beforehand, but was badly caught out on my very first Sunday. We had been assigned to a Presbyterian church in a wealthy suburb of New York. Julian made the initial mistake of commenting on and asking about the splendid books that were laid out on coffee tables by our hosts. She quickly realized she had blundered:

the books were there for show, and no one had read them! My own blunder — though Julian felt it had been salutary for some — was to have preached on sin and forgiveness. As I emerged from the vestry afterwards I was seized by the lapels of my jacket, and an angry elder growled at me, "What do you think you are doing, calling us sinners? Don't you know I built this church?"

Much of the six-week tour gave us the experience of the generosity and warmth of well-heeled New England church congregations — the only ones that could afford these lavish fees for visiting preachers — whose white-gloved stewards asked me unfamiliar questions such as, "Do you like to have the lights dimmed for the benediction?" But toward the end, after Julian had left me to return home to the children, I felt I came closer to some of the social realities of the USA. One of the invitations was to a black Baptist church in Brooklyn. As we were about to go up to the stage from the green room — which is what the church arrangements felt like — the minister sought to encourage me by saying, "You can preach to us for an hour, an hour and a half.... we like it here, we are not in a hurry." My standard twenty-minute address began to burn in my pocket and I wondered what would happen when I had finished delivering it. But I need not have worried. I found myself confronted by a huge auditorium with a sea of black faces, already warming up with a gospel singer and ready to interject their "Hallelujahs" and their "Praise the Lords!" at the slightest invitation to do so. Once I began preaching, I realized we would go very slowly indeed: the responses were frequent and enthusiastic, and were working up to a veritable climax of uninhibited religiosity. For a while, I was exhilarated, and played along with the mood, giving the people plenty of opportunity to respond. But the experience was also alarming. I felt as if I were sitting at a great organ, and could go on pulling out the stops as long as I wished. It gave me a feeling of power that must surely be dangerous. If one could so easily work up this enthusiasm, what limit was there to the damage one might do? And how strong the temptation to stay within the safe limits of their approval! The minister told me afterwards that he had very serious problems of alcoholism among the congregation; but he dared not mention it in a sermon, or he would lose his job!

By chance I met an Anglican priest from Chicago, who invited me to his own parish and handed me a return ticket for the plane (my first experience of jet travel, which was still new in Britain). What he wanted to show me was the "Chicago Reading Room." There were a number of denominations offering refuge and food to the many vagrants and jobless; but they all did so, he told me, on condition that the recipients attended evangelistic talks, meetings, and prayers. But this one, sponsored by the mayor, did none of that. There was indeed a "reading room," with newspapers and some books; there was also a set of showers, a canteen, a job center, and a medical center, indeed it was a forerunner of the day centers for the homeless that I was to be involved with years later in London. As a priest, he assured me this was doing more for the men's spiritual health and well-being, and was a more potent Christian example, than all the preaching and converting that was going on in other centers. And I believed him.

He then asked me to join him on his yacht for a sail around the bay. We were a mixed party, which included (for some reason) Alec Vidler, the well-known and forthright dean of King's College Cambridge, and also a distinguished black pharmacologist. The wind was so strong that no other craft were out except our host's, which was in fact the largest sailing boat in the harbor. When we turned back — to the intense relief of those of our party who were feeling dreadfully seasick (Alec Vidler had turned distinctly green) — he suggested we all have lunch together at the Yacht Club. When we got home, his telephone began ringing almost continuously. Outraged members of the Yacht Club (all white) were demanding why he had brought "this nigger" in to lunch. And the same experience of undisguised racism continued for me when next day I was invited by the same pharmacologist for a drink at his apartment. When I arrived there, to my surprise he did not ask me in — it was an apartment block in an elegant part of the city — but immediately took me to a residents' bar. And then I realized why: he wanted to be seen with a white man on his own ground. Such was the state of American race relations at that time. Thanks to my fearless host, I had seen something of the reality behind the screen of comfortable respectability that had surrounded me during most of my tour.

CHAPTER 4

Apprenticeship: Oxford and Jerusalem

With my academic record, there never seemed to be any question of allowing me to proceed to another post in a parish. Inquiries began to come in from Oxford; and in 1962 I found myself appointed to a newly created research studentship (Christ Church's idiosyncratic name for fellowship) at Oxford's largest and (at least in its own eyes) most prestigious college, with a cathedral within its precincts and a dean (Cuthbert Simpson) whose bluff American good sense and humanity gave a distinct character to the college at that time. He, too, was steadfastly convinced of my abilities, and was one of those who secured for me the commission to write a *Companion to the New Testament* for the Oxford and Cambridge University Presses — a task that occupied most of the years I spent at Christ Church. The book was published in 1970, a year after I left Oxford for Canterbury. He became one of our firmest and most hospitable friends, offering the deanery, unasked, for receptions after a family christening and a marriage. He was ready with advice, and gave it in a refreshingly humorous and pragmatic idiom. When I went to him in some distress, fearing that my widowed father was becoming entangled with an exploitative housekeeper, he leaned over his desk and said, with apparent seriousness, "Can't you *poison* her?"

The seven years I spent at Christ Church were an extraordinary gift for a young man in his thirties. At the High Table and in the Common Room I found myself sitting next to men (they were still all men in the 'sixties) of outstanding quality and distinction — Roy Harrod (author of the first major biography of John Maynard Keynes), Lord Cherwell (Frederick Lindemann, Churchill's indispensable boffin), Alex Russell (who had worked with Rutherford splitting the atom in Cambridge), E. R. Dodds (Gilbert Murray's successor as Regius Professor of Greek), now retired but maintaining a discreet presence in the Common Room, and many others. Not that I always felt at ease with these, or indeed with most of my colleagues. Whether it was shyness, or whether it was the recurring consciousness of being, in the end, in some sense an amateur, I had an unfortunate impulse to try to justify my presence by apparent intelligence of conversation, always in fear of being betrayed by insecure foundations of knowledge.

At the same time I had some wonderful friends and supporters, particularly two of those who were arguably among the most brilliant men in the college. One was the Regius Professor of Greek at the time, Hugh Lloyd-Jones, whom I had first met when I invited him to give a talk on the Third Programme during my time at the BBC. His script had required considerable editing, his manner of delivering it had to be severely controlled (he liked to thump the table and twist about in his chair in a manner totally incompatible with the requirements of a radio studio), and I remember I waited nervously for the verdict of my fellow producers on whether he was an acceptable broadcaster at all. He gained their hesitant acceptance; but he was aware that he owed this to my efforts as much as to his own, and knowing of my early achievements as a classical scholar he formed a respect for me that reciprocated mine for him. We remained firm friends all the time I was at Oxford. Of course he regretted that I had strayed away from classics into theology (he was unashamedly anticlerical); but he acknowledged that since I spent most of my time working on a text that was in Greek, I was a colleague with whom he had something in common — unlike those who worked in the field of Christian doctrine, who to his mind were wasting such intellectual gifts as they possessed in the study of something that did not exist.

My other close friend and mentor was Henry Chadwick, who was at the time Regius Professor of Theology and lived in the college in Tom Quad. He was not only an astonishingly learned theologian; he had also read music at Cambridge and was a fine pianist — he used to find time to come to our house on Hinksey Hill and play violin and piano sonatas with me. Without his advice and encouragement I would have floundered more than I did. I could not accept the program he proposed to me: he wanted me to do a critical edition of the text of an early Greek Father that happened not to have received full treatment by anyone else. This idea ran up against my old instinct to find some academic work that had immediate relevance — this one could indeed be called a dry-as-dust project — and left him puzzled by my lack of enthusiasm (or was it by my amateurishness?). But for a time I placed before him drafts of my first efforts at reviewing academic books. "Oh, you can't say that," he told me, "that poor man would be dreadfully hurt." And he went on to give me a piece of advice that I have always treasured. "There is just one way of pointing out that someone is wrong without giving offence. Just say, 'I cannot agree with Mr. so-and-so that....' The reader will get the point, and all will be well between you." For writing reviews the principle was invaluable, and I have tried to adhere to it ever since. Had I applied it also to argument and conversation I would have avoided many occasions when my ripostes were seen as offensive: it has only been in recent years that I have been able to soften my reputation for not being able to suffer fools gladly.

My post being a research fellowship, there was opportunity to travel if my work required it. After my first three years I had virtually completed my *Companion* in respect of the letters of St. Paul, but was perplexed as to how to tackle the gospels. The secretary of the University Press, Colin Roberts, who had commissioned me to write the book for the Oxford and Cambridge University Presses, was a papyrologist and firmly believed in the value of seeing for oneself where things came from: even papyrus fragments from the sands of Egypt might be more intelligible to one who had seen the sites where they had been found. Accordingly he persuaded the Press to finance a short visit to the Holy Land for me and Julian in 1964, and encouraged me to make a longer stay if I could. There were two good reasons for doing so: knowledge of the physical background of events recorded in the New Testament would often illuminate the text in surprising ways; and the Ecole Biblique, founded by, and still the home of, a distinguished line of French Dominican scholars, had one of the best libraries in the world for biblical and archaeological studies.

So in 1966 we bought a secondhand VW minibus, stowed as many of our requirements as we could into its recesses (I thought we were full to capacity when Julian produced five Christmas puddings that she insisted must come with us — and she was right, they were invaluable social assets in the Jerusalem winter!) and set off with our three daughters who were all under the age of nine. We crossed Europe by easy stages as far as Venice, where we boarded a Greek ship bound for Beirut. The minibus was lifted up by a crane and simply parked on the deck, so that we were able to go and sit in it when we wanted to make ourselves a cup of tea. This was not the only sign of an apparently casual approach to safety in the ship. Nothing seemed to be securely tied down, and I was thankful we had a smooth crossing (by no means assured in late September). When we arrived at Beirut I naively thought the car would simply be lifted off again just as it had been hoisted on. But no one else seemed to think this, and I found I was being pestered for a large sum of money before we could leave. Still naive, I thought I might wear them down if I went on protesting, and this time I was right: after about twenty-four hours, during which we obstinately refused to leave the ship, the car was suddenly attached to a crane and we found ourselves free to continue across Lebanon, through Syria and into Jordan. It was only when we were preparing to return nine months later that I was told that in the Levant no one ever dreamed of trying to load or unload a vehicle without an agent.

The frontiers could have been a problem, in that my Hebrew Bible, for example, would raise suspicions in Arab countries neighboring Israel, and there could have been prolonged searches. But that was to reckon without the impact on the guards of three small children in the back of the car. At once there were smiles and greetings, turning sad and sympathetic when they saw they were all girls. "It is the will of Allah," they said, with evident compassion; and it was hard to convince them we were entirely happy with our family of daughters. Then they would gaily wave us through the checkpoints.

And so, now in Jordan (for what we now call the West Bank and East Jerusalem then belonged to the Hashemite Kingdom), we reached the foot of the Mount of Olives below the Old City. At that point the car, which had performed perfectly throughout the long journey, suddenly died on us. What on earth were we to do? Our family and all our necessary belongings were in it, the hour was late and the children were tired and becoming fractious. Our perplexity paralyzed us for some time. Eventually we tried to start the car again. It spluttered into action and conveyed us, with frequent hiccoughs, up the last half mile into the Old City (the cause of the trouble remained a mystery, though it recurred from time to time; years later it was found to be a metallic particle that had got into the petrol, apparently when we filled up in Lebanon).

When we arrived in the Anglican Cathedral compound of St. George's there was a mixed welcome. The archbishop, Campbell MacInnes, had generously offered us the use of a flat that was part of the ground floor of his house beside the cathedral. What he had not told us was that the flat was normally occupied by one of his staff, who was away in England for six months, had no children of his own and was known to be house-proud. Seeing us bring three small children into those carefully tended surroundings, some of the residents of the compound began shaking their heads and muttering — particularly as they had a strong impression that the archbishop had never warned Canon Alun Morris, the occupant, that it was a young family to whom he had offered the flat. Fortunately, in this respect, our children were exemplary. In the somewhat formal dining room of St. George's Hostel, where we had some of our meals, they were quiet, polite, and respectful; and it was soon noticed that they had inherited their mother's instinctive sense of social ease and propriety, which meant that our visitors always received a reassuring welcome. As for Campbell himself, he adored children (he shared a birthday with our second daughter and established an immediate complicity with her), as did his wife, who had been a surgeon and relieved us of all medical anxieties. Their welcome was spontaneous, their sense of fun hilarious, and their support and friendship lasted all through our stay.

Thus we found ourselves established in a secure and (eventually) welcoming British enclave in the Old City of Jerusalem. The children were young enough for their education to be more a matter of finding ways they could pass their time happily and usefully than of having any fixed program or syllabus. Marina, aged eight, spent the first few months learning cross-stitch with a group of Palestinian refugee girls under the tuition of a partly Russian lady who quickly detected her abilities and ordered the Arab girls to emulate her — causing her, inevitably, some unpopularity. She then went to the big convent school run by the Dames de Sion, where the only two languages were Arabic and French. Sensibly, the nuns did not try to teach her French systematically, given she would only be there a few months, but read and talked to her enough to give her a feel for the language, which gave her a good start later in life. Helen, aged six, went to the equivalent of a dame's school run for British and American children by a formidable lady who took charge single-handed of about a dozen children of widely different ages and gave each of them a surprisingly appropriate education. Christian, aged four, went to an Italian kindergarten, where the only languages spoken were Arabic and Italian. But she went in company with the youngest daughter of Desmond Tutu, who was doing some postgraduate work at St. George's College, and so long as they were together they seemed perfectly happy, not least because the nuns' policy appeared to be spanking the boys and giving sweets to the girls.

All in all, not much was learned academically (though the "Dame's School" did do some serious education), but the experience of living at close quarters with the Arab population, becoming familiar with the crowded streets of the Old City, and above all travelling around in a landscape which, before 1967, had barely changed since biblical times, left a profound impression on all the children — as it did on me and Julian. And for me the lectures of the brilliant and humane director, Pierre Benoit, the archaeological visits conducted by him and other Dominicans, and excursions such as that to Qumran with Roland de Vaux (one of the first scholars to work on the Dead Sea Scrolls) gave the fresh impetus to my New Testament work that I had come to find. Many years later I came across a book by the youngest daughter of C. R. Ashbee (the founder of the Guild of Handicrafts), who was engaged as architect and planner by General Allenby after Jerusalem had been taken from the Turks in 1917. Ashbee worked in Jerusalem for three years, and took with him his family, which consisted of his wife and four daughters under the age of ten. The parallel of his venture with our own was striking; and reading Felicity Ashbee's book I realized how little had changed in the half century between them. We experienced exactly the same courtesy and hospitality as they had, exactly the same sense of participation in an ancient civilization that had retained its traditional values, its love of its own land, and its traditional excellences with a faithfulness that at times put us to shame.[1]

There was one occasion when we drove to the moon-like desert landscape of Wadi Rum, where there was a small fort manned by Bedouin soldiers in their long khaki skirts. I wanted to see the Nabatean inscription that was high up on the mountain by a spring. Would they tell us how to get there? By no means: they insisted on one of them walking there with us. Julian made this record of our visit:

> We arrived in this strange, vast land, and very soon were in sight of the Desert Patrol, tall and beautifully dressed, alert, with their exquisite camels beside them. They welcomed us and said we could leave the children with them while we walked up to "the fountain." It was hot going. One of the men came with us to get the pure water for their mint tea. The sand was white, and there were tall desert plants, grey and fleshy, growing out of rocks. Half way up I said to Anthony, "I do hope the children are safe! Maybe we should not have left them." But those men of the Desert Patrol were so straight, like something from Lawrence of Arabia's time.... We followed our companion into the wonderful coolness of the precious spring water, as it ran do wn the dark, smooth rocks. It was a blessing in itself, shaded from the merciless heat of the sun by another rock. Our Desert Patrol man had filled his kettle for their tea, and we turned back, a little loth to leave this place,

---

1. See *Some Writings of Julain Harvey*, section 2, pp. 173-76.

this fountain with its Nabatean inscription. When we got back, there was Christian (our four-year-old daughter) on the back of a sitting camel, one most beautifully brushed, pale in colour, and obviously known to be gentle. A Desert Patrol soldier was near her. The others were playing a game, a sort of draughts in the sand, with small pieces of clean dry camel dung. They were being shown how to do it, and were so absorbed that they scarcely looked up. Then we too were included, and, with such courtesy, given the herb tea made from the pure water. How precious that meeting was!

Apart from travel and study, I was given privileged insight into the arcane ecclesiastical world of the Old City. On important festivals it was the custom for heads of churches to pay a ceremonial visit to one another, for which purpose Campbell, our archbishop, invited me to act as his chaplain. We would set off as a small deputation, preceded by our *kawass* wearing a fez and striking the pavement with an imposing official staff. At each patriarchate we would be received in exactly the same way: we would be ushered into a reception room with chairs all around the walls, along with similar groups from other churches, and would invariably be served with a tiny cup of coffee, a thimbleful of liqueur, and a chocolate wrapped in colored silver paper (these Campbell always secreted into the pocket of his cassock for use later when he would be the host himself — perhaps this was what they all did, in which case the same chocolates will have gone round and round!). The prelates sat together at one end of the room, and conversation was formal and (in my case) inevitably stilted, but could be significant. "Not good weather today?" "No, bad weather coming from Egypt" — which was code for President Nasser being up to no good.

As for relations between the churches, they inherited an age-old distrust of one another. On the evening of Good Friday Campbell invited me to walk with him as his chaplain in the Abyssinians' procession around the roof of St. Helena's chapel in the Church of the Holy Sepulchre. This was an ancient ritual known as "Searching for the Body," and consisted of the white-robed clergy slowly working their way around the roof with chanting and drums, the procession being a snake eating its own tail, the patriarch leading it being on the heels of those who came at the end. By now it was dark, and the ceremony was well under way, when we became aware of brickbats falling on us from the battlements above. I felt someone's hands on my shoulders pulling me abruptly into a doorway, and in seconds the roof was completely empty — clearly this was an interruption that people were used to! It transpired that the Copts, who owned the adjacent rooftop, had objected to a cross which they alleged had been placed in their territory by the Abyssinians, and had retaliated by disrupting the ritual. Next day the Muslim governor (following Ottoman precedent) called on the Coptic patriarch to demand an explanation. The patriarch, he was told, was indisposed and could not see him. Such episodes were not uncommon. The Latin (i.e. Catholic) procession into the Grotto at Bethlehem on Christmas Eve might be held up by Greek Orthodox clergy on some pretext that proper protocol had not been observed. The Muslim governor of Bethlehem would be summoned to mediate. If he failed, a further summons would be conveyed to the governor of Jerusalem, (only five miles away), whose word would be accepted as final, and the procession, having waited several hours with guttering candles, would eventually be allowed to move on. And there were other sources of friction in church life. We used sometimes to attend services in the Assyrian church below the Mount of Olives, where the language was deemed to be very close to the Aramaic spoken by Jesus and where there was a particularly friendly and welcoming local congregation. One day, on an important festival, we noticed that the evidently well-liked patriarch was absent. When I asked Campbell about it, he replied, "Ah yes, it is very sad. You see, he bribed the wrong man."

Julian and the children had equally vivid experiences. She wrote a short talk on them for the BBC, which was accepted and paid for but never broadcast — perhaps due to some political pressure?

... and from Egypt, Coptic pilgrims in grey blue robes. I shall never forget the sight of them in the Church of the Holy Sepulchre curled up on the scaffolding high above the Tomb itself, hours beforehand waiting for the Holy Fire. There was always a trickle of Christians from the West and at Easter and Christmas they'd fill the comfortable hotels the Jordanians had built in their new city outside the walls. On Friday afternoons we'd see them on the Via Dolorosa, led in prayer by a Franciscan. Sometimes there was an evening walk across the old city to the Garden of Gethsemane.

As for the Tourist Police, the longer I was there the more I admired them. When excitement was at its height during the great religious festivals and people pushed one another or fainted, it was these men who would stop the pushing and miraculously lift those who had fainted high over the heads of the crowd. I even saw one obligingly catch the handkerchief of an old Greek pilgrim and drop it for her in the holy water left from the ceremony of the washing of the feet.

Like me, our children loved the Old City, they had their favourite haunts. The youngest liked to jump down the narrow steps of David's Street where the endless Barakat cousins sold cross-stitch dresses, Bedouin coffee jugs, and the carpets brought by Eastern pilgrims to pay their way. Marina's was her special coin man, where she spent her pocket money. Helen's was the Jerusalem pottery where each day the young Armenian who ran it had some new and exciting design based on local mosaics or frescos. On these occasions, when I had all three children with me, we would have to stop to watch the great mill stones crushing the oil from sesame seeds. That is how they made tahini, a sticky stuff rather like peanut butter, the basis of Arab salads. We had to stop too, at the pastry shop, to see the pastry cook throw out his dough until it was the size of a pillowcase, smooth and thin. We'd wait 'til the boy drew one of them out of the blazing oven — by now it was folded and filled with walnuts and honey. This we'd eat in our fingers from a large pewter tray, then we would continue our way along the narrow souks, the children shouting out if they saw one of the Little Sisters of Jesus in their blue serge, their favourite of the many religious orders that live in the Old City.

In Jerusalem we were in the centre of two worlds. Pilgrims came from London and Paris, from Isfahan and Ethiopia, and the authorities of the city accepted them with the same friendly welcome, the same quiet reverence for the holy places of Christianity and of Islam. I hope some of this spirit will continue in the Old City now the Jews can worship again at the Wailing Wall. But will those vast numbers of poor Eastern pilgrims still come to Jerusalem? Will a modern Western state like Israel tolerate these poor peasants, sleeping in their buses, lighting their kerosene stoves, waiting on girders and rooftops hours before their ceremonies begin? I hope so.

We had planned for a six months' stay; but toward the end the dean of St. George's Cathedral had to return to England on compassionate leave and I was asked to stay a further two months and take his place until he returned. Canon Morris (who turned out to be a welcoming friend despite all that had been said about him when we arrived) was expected any moment, so we moved into the dean's flat in St. George's College (part of the compound) and I looked after the cathedral as best I could for the next two months. The plan was then to leave in June, sailing from Haifa, where I was to accompany the archbishop and preach at an ordination service. But rumors of the impending six-day war were everywhere. The consulate advised us to leave without delay. We hurriedly packed our things and drove towards Damascus — seeing the Great Mosque was an experience we had deliberately put off until our journey home. But all the advice we received was to avoid delay. When I called at the hotel in Damascus where we would have spent the night I explained we had been told we should not stay after all. The man at the desk simply nodded silently — as eloquent a confirmation of the consular advice as I could have asked for. We left the car in charge of some small boys and made a dash to the mosque, to have at least a glimpse of it before we left. We then hastened on to cross into Lebanon on our way to Beirut — just in time, for the very next day there was an explosion at the Syrian frontier, with the inevitable sequel that no one was allowed in or out of the country until further notice. Had we not left when we did we would have been virtually under house arrest for several weeks. As it was, the 1967 war, which was to change the face of Jerusalem forever, began while we were on an Italian ship bound for Venice. To my shame, I have never been back to Jerusalem since. Indeed, Julian and I soon realized that it was going to be much more difficult to do so, and, bereft of our hope to return quite soon, we found consolation in the birth of our fourth daughter, Victoria, six years after that of her youngest sister. One of the names we gave her was Petra, keeping alive a particularly vivid memory of our travels in the Middle East.

Back in Oxford for the autumn term of 1967 I found that the Jerusalem experience had indeed stimulated new understandings of the gospels, and I made rapid progress with my *Companion*. And there were further experiences to do with the ancient world. Julian's father had been a teacher at King Edward's School, Birmingham until shortly before World War Two, and there his family had become friends with E. R. Dodds and his wife. Dodds (always known by his initials: I never heard his Christian name) was then professor of Greek and only later moved to Oxford when he became Regius Professor in succession to Gilbert Murray. The Regius Professorship carried a fellowship ("studentship") at Christ Church, where he received a less than warm welcome: many in the college had supported a likely candidate from their own number and did not believe that Dodds was up to the job; in addition they knew that, as a Northern Irishman, he had sympathies with Sinn Fein, which made him highly suspect in that inherently conservative institution. As a result, the Dodds's withdrew from most aspects of social life; they lived outside Oxford in a house with a large garden (which they loved passionately) and were seldom seen in public together. When the McMasters moved to Oxford during the war the Doddses naturally rejoiced in the presence of their old friends and they saw much of each other. Dodds's tenure of the prestigious professorship in fact turned out to be a distinguished one, and after his retirement he felt sufficiently at home in Christ Church to appear regularly for lunch in the Common Room. For me it was the renewal of contact with a former teacher: I had attended his classes with enthusiasm when an undergraduate. He had by now become a regular lecturer on Swan's Hellenic Cruises, and it was he who persuaded them to take me on as chaplain/lecturer.

This I found to be no sinecure. The preparation needed for lecturing on ancient sites that I had never seen meant many hours studying archeological reports and scholarly guide books, and fresh demands might always be made during the cruise itself if there had to be a change of course owing to bad weather and a new set of sites to be introduced. The passengers also kept the lecturers up to the mark: there were always some daunting ladies with purple-rinsed hair who had been on some seventeen cruises before, and one knew they were carefully comparing one's performance with that of previous lecturers. But here my gifts as an amateur came into play. I was adept at bluffing my way out of situations where my ignorance might be exposed, and a certain natural eloquence and persuasiveness with which I am gifted convinced even my more skeptical hearers.

Julian too had a part to play — for lecturers' wives were always courteously invited to accompany their husbands (female lecturers were a rarity at the time) and asked to do duty in the ship's library between ports of call. On one of our cruises there was a shortage of Byzantine scholars, and in Istanbul a lecturer was required to be stationed in the church of the Chora outside the city walls, explaining to successive parties of cruise passengers the significance of the mosaics and frescoes. These are outstanding monuments to the brief period of transition from Byzantine to Renaissance-inspired art, which was cut short by the fall of Constantinople in 1453. Julian was well qualified to fill the role, having done some work on Byzantine history at Oxford and with her exceptional aptitude for anything to do with the history of art. Her only difficulty was with some of the names. For weeks before, she had gone to sleep at night wearily rehearsing the name Theodore Metochites, the emperor responsible for the building of this remarkable church. When it came to the point she played her part to general admiration — and we still had time for a visit to the great mosques inside the city walls: I found Hagia Sophia an unforgettable architectural experience that fully justified Edward Gibbons' lavish description of it in *Decline and Fall*.

Unforgettable in another way was the cruise down the Bosporus. I had been carefully instructed by Henry Chadwick (a seasoned Swan's chaplain/lecturer) how to perform the ritual of throwing a wreath on to the sea as we passed the Anzac beaches: "Make sure you give it a spin with your wrist, otherwise it may come back and hit the ship!" More difficult was the assignment of being on the bridge in the early morning as we steamed up the narrows: I was supposed to identify the towns, ancient and modern, as we passed them on either side for the benefit of any passengers who were listening at that hour. As we crept along in the mist nothing seemed quite to match the descriptions I had carefully studied in the guide books, and the Turkish captain seemed unable to help me as I tried to discern the outline of some of the lesser-known sites. Excellent men, the captains, but not always quite on my wave-length. On another occasion I was on the bridge steaming round the Bay of Naples. Most of the passengers had disembarked for an excursion to Pompeii; for those who remained on the ship there was a cruise around the bay with a lecturer on the bridge indicating points of interest over the loud speakers. We were just approaching Capri, and I was getting into my stride talking about the Emperor Tiberius and his collection of be-jeweled ornamental fish in the fish ponds, when I felt a tug at my arm, and the captain was growling into my ear, "Do not forget to mention the funicular railway."

During these seven years at Oxford I could not have asked for a more stimulating or supportive environment for the first stage of an academic career, or to be better poised to obtain a long-term post in the university (though it happened that none became available in all the seven years I was there). But the same ambivalence continued to haunt me: Was it right to devote all my energies to academic work, remote from the trials and tribulations of less privileged people? Of course there was some teaching — not very much of it in my case: it was only later that I realized that offering help and guidance to young people at a questing period in their lives is as responsible and valuable an occupation as anyone could wish for. There had also been a chance to travel: the year I spent in Jerusalem was, at the very least, a broadening experience and resulted in subsequent work with experts on the Middle East at the British Council of Churches. But even this did not seem enough. I had already had two years as a part-time chaplain at the Warneford psychiatric hospital; restless, I took on some limited pastoral work at a women's college, and got involved with issues arising from clergy training. I was by now convinced that theology is an academic discipline that should always have some bearing on the living of a Christian life. It followed that, in the training of those called to be priests, it must not be treated simply as an academic qualification that, once obtained, could be left on the shelf. It could, and surely must, be taught in such a way that it would continue to influence faith and practice for the rest of a minister's life. I was ready for a chance to put this conviction to the test, and on the urging of Sydney Evans, its dean, I was appointed by King's College London as principal (or "warden") of its new fourth year course for ordinands at St. Augustine's College, Canterbury.

CHAPTER 5

Experimentation: Canterbury

B y way of making a break between Oxford and Canterbury and giving me time to reflect on what I had undertaken, I took the family (our youngest, Victoria, was now one year old) to stay for six weeks in a farmhouse in the village of Taizé in Burgundy. Taizé was already becoming known as an innovative monastic community. I had visited it first in the early fifties, when it was still quite small and tentative. Founded by a Swiss Protestant pastor soon after the Second World War, who had been joined by a small number of exceptionally gifted men — an architect, an artist, a potter, and several others — it had grown, by the time I first knew it, into a community of thirty or so Brothers (some of whom were working in small groups in some of the poorest places in the world). Frère Roger, the prior, had acquired a disused château in the village and had been permitted by the Roman Catholic authorities to use the tiny romanesque church for their services. Guest quarters were extremely limited: when I took Julian there soon after our marriage we stayed in the house of a farmer's wife who had just one available room with a bucket to catch the rainwater that came through the roof in thunderstorms. Meals were outside in the courtyard, where Madame prepared snails for dinner, always attended by a faithful duck. The toilet was a noisome hut in the yard. But the beauty of the place, the informal simplicity of the Brothers and the vigor and musical excellence of their worship were an inspiration to us and to many others and have since penetrated into church life in many parts of the world.

In the course of the student unrest in Paris in the sixties, young people on their way to holidays in the south of France, began turning aside to Taizé, and, once there, put up their tents and stayed. A new church had to be built — discreetly wedged into the hillside — to accommodate them, and the visitors rapidly grew into a throng of thousands, with a number of the Brothers detailed to take care of them, which they did through training young volunteers to take responsibility for practical arrangements. Encouraged to stay for a week, the young people were grouped in sections, some opting for silent retreat, some for regular discussion and study, and some to join working parties preparing the space for still more visitors. Soon notices were appearing in little-known languages from Eastern Europe, and young people began to arrive from distant parts of the world. The community, which had been founded as an ecumenical venture to promote the unity of the church, found itself the center of massive international pilgrimages of young people and had to adjust its life accordingly. Yet it retained the essential simplicity and transparency of its life and worship, which were the qualities that had attracted so many visitors in the first place.

It was after the new church had been built that we came with our family in 1969. It was a building that aimed to combine beauty with provisionality. The outside was sited so as to be inconspicuous; inside, it was a large open space, with no chairs over most of the floor, but with a few rows of steps along the sides that provided simple seating for those who did not wish to squat or kneel on the roughly carpeted floor. The level of lighting was low, with small stained glass windows, mostly designed by Frère Eric, giving a glow of color to the concrete walls. Large numbers of night-lights and candles made for a numinous atmosphere, which conveyed itself instantly to the large number of young people kneeling or squatting on the space round the Brothers, whose own area for prayer and worship was marked out only by traces of greenery or miniature box hedges. The prior liked always to have a handful of small children around him during services, and our own children were among those who frequently had this experience. This custom continued until his death by assassination in 2009; indeed there were small children around him at the moment when a mentally deranged woman approached and stabbed him fatally with a knife. Those same children, even after the trauma of being literally spattered with his blood, returned early next morning, of their own volition, to sit next to his successor, who had been nominated long before and immediately took his place at the head of the Brothers. This spontaneous gesture by these very young witnesses of the murder was one of the factors that helped the community to recover from the shock of the murder and continue its life as before.

During our stay in the village we gradually got to know some of the Brothers, who became long-term friends. The artist Frère Eric began to visit us regularly for English lessons, which took the form of reading Beatrix Potter with the children. Later, in the United States, he was dismayed to find that the word "Pattypan," as in the title of one of her books, was unknown in America! Meanwhile I had a chance to discuss my plans for theological education with others in the community and to broaden my own spirituality through daily attending their worship. Later, in the college, I introduced some elements both of the Taizé community life (such as taking meals in small groups for the discussion of important issues) and of their worship. Some of the students ridiculed my attachment to this French-speaking monastic experiment, but many of them saw possibilities in it, and I was able to take enthusiastic groups of them there in the following years. One of these, in a private session with the prior, asked for a definition of "priest" — doubtless expecting something authoritative and ecclesiastical. I shall never forget his reply: *un homme à l'écoute*, "a person who is always listening."

Strengthened and inspired by this experience, we moved to our impressive, if inconvenient, Butterfield house in Canterbury. St Augustine's was founded as a Missionary College in 1848 amid the ruins of what had been one of the major religious houses in England. Its Abbey church had been begun in Saxon times and was on a scale comparable with that of the cathedral just a few hundred yards away. Of the medieval buildings little remained except the guests' dining hall and the thirteenth-century Fyndon Gateway, the original entry to the monastery. This contained a fine room in its upper story that was allegedly slept in by Queen Elizabeth and Charles II, as well as by

Charles I when he was returning to London with his bride Henrietta
Maria. The room was still intact — we called it the Gateway Chamber — and provided a dignified meeting room for the new college.
The other college buildings were designed by Butterfield around a
courtyard, one side of which was formed by the Tudor wall of a garden created by Henry VIII when the buildings were briefly used as a
royal palace. There were two chapels, one above the other; the lower
one became a memorial to the missionaries who passed through the
college, many of whom perished from disease in Africa and two of
whom (inscribed in red letters) were martyred. Next to it was the
Warden's Lodge, of which the main ground floor room was described
by a former occupant as "the finest clergyman's study in the Anglican
Communion" — which (having been warden himself) he had reason
to know, since after the Missionary College was blitzed and closed
during the war it was reopened in 1952 as the Central College of the
Anglican Communion, a house of short-term study for clergy from
all over the world. It was a splendid room, too large, I thought, for my
own use, and it became our drawing room, the most attractive one
we have ever had. The large first floor room, which previously had
been the family living room, we made into our bedroom, and there,
one night, Julian had a vivid experience of seeing a small maid in an
apron and linen cap stoking up the (no longer existing) fire — we
had a number of similar, but not alarming, paranormal experiences in
various parts of the house. It was an awkward house, with a number
of small rooms clustered around, below and above the two large ones,
connected by two daunting stone staircases. But by dint of painting
all the walls white (which must have been very far from Butterfield's
intentions) we were able to make it into an agreeable family home,
where our four daughters had the space for many childhood enter-
prises, such as creating a poultry yard for bantams and ducks in the
narrow strip of garden separating our house from the road: the crow-
ing of our cocks so close to other houses must have often roused our
neighbors to start the day unusually early — but none complained.

The windows at the back of the house had a fine view of Canterbury Cathedral — we were indeed only just outside the Cathedral
Close. Relations with the clergy there were quite cordial, but ever

since the nineteenth century the fact of not being part of the cathedral community had created a certain distrust of the college, which we inherited even in our own time; and it was reinforced when the dean came and spoke at a question-and-answer session with the students: he found himself taken less seriously than he was accustomed to, and after one or two unashamedly irreverent questions (such as "What has the cathedral ever done for anyone?") I had to bring the meeting to an end and revive him with whisky in our house. The news travelled rapidly around the close and we sensed a coldness from its residents that lasted for most of our time. Nevertheless we received some help and support. We were allowed to take part in some of the cathedral services, and received favored treatment at the enthronement of a new archbishop — an occasion which I remember vividly for quite other reasons. The cathedral authorities had hit on a brilliant scheme for giving lunch to distinguished visitors before the service, which was in the afternoon. Since they would be bound to be coming from London, they could be served lunch on the train! Only a few days before the ceremony it was realized that there might be some coming from the opposite direction, across the Channel. So what about their lunch? At short notice I was asked if I could provide it; and we held a lunch party in our house which was attended by, among others, a Swedish monk and the Abbot of Bec.

I placed the venerable abbot next to me, and tried to explore what I thought were appropriate subjects to do with spirituality and the monastic life. I soon found I was making no headway at all: the only thing he wanted to talk about was English food, and in particular Julian's cooking. All the time I was keeping my eye on the clock, since the party had to be in the cathedral in good time, and when we got to the dessert all seemed to be going according to plan. But then, to my dismay, Julian pointed to an array of cheeses on the sideboard and suggested that our guests might like to help themselves — an extra course that I had not allowed for! The abbot's eyes lit up, and he helped himself to a portion of every cheese on offer, and placed on his plate a veritable tower of biscuits to eat with them. I soon realized that if we were to wait for him to finish before moving to the drawing room for coffee, there was no way I could get them all to the cathedral

in time, and in desperation I asked the Swedish monk to sit next to
him until he had finished. I then shepherded the other guests out of
the room, and contrived to have the whole party ready in the cathedral cloisters for the police to search them before going in (it was a
period of high alert following an act of terrorism by the IRA). There
they began to feel grateful for having been given a good lunch, since
they were subjected to a long wait in the icy wind that often blew
upon us in East Kent. The abbot complained loudly, even though I
was carrying his case for him (it was exceedingly heavy), saying he
would never come to such an occasion again. Since he was already of
a good age, with a girth that hardly suggested a healthy life-style, it
seemed unlikely that he would live long enough to have the opportunity, since archbishops of Canterbury do not normally retire after less
than ten years; but I too had left by the time Robert Runcie retired
and I do not know whether in fact the abbot came again, though the
Abbey of Bec would certainly have been represented, given its close
association with Canterbury ever since the time of Archbishop Lanfranc, who had himself been its abbot in the eleventh century.

I had little idea, when I accepted the task of starting a new college
for ordinands from King's College London, what a culture shock it
would be. These young graduates were a very different proposition
from the students I had got to know and made friends with at Oxford. The great majority came from modest backgrounds; many of
them had been the bright boy in a working-class family and had been
exempted by their mothers from domestic tasks and duties, and so
given a sense of entitlement to preferential treatment. In addition,
the student world by the end of the 'sixties had become turbulent.
Students clamored for rights to have their say in every aspect of college management, and even the small body of forty or so at Canterbury would insist on endless meetings over relatively trivial issues,
sometimes including long discussions about whether the meeting
was "quorate." All this made the difficulty of leading them toward
a new understanding of Christian ministry one which took me and
most of my staff by surprise. Only one of us had any previous experience of the King's culture, and the students themselves, who had
known each other for the previous three years, presented a united

and often obstinate front in face of the challenges we were trying to confront them with. None of this was I prepared for (I have to blame Sydney Evans for not making me more aware of it beforehand: he may have thought I would be put off and decline the job!), and the first year's students undoubtedly suffered from our fumbling approach, even though some have since become friends and would now say that the year was an important and formative time for them.

In many ways Canterbury proved to be an enriching experience for me and my family. I still held the conviction which had led me to accept the challenge in the first place, namely that the justification for all my academic theology must lie in proving it to be of application to the realities of daily life. At Canterbury we were free to devise a course would force the students (and us) to bring the theology that had been learned — our whole understanding of the Christian faith — to bear on the realities of modern life. Students went in groups into some stressful environments — the mental hospital, social work, a prison. Back in college, the group would explore together its members' reactions (a searching process in itself) and then look at some basic Christian propositions. After the experience of meeting an inmate in the prison who was apparently resistant to any attempt at reform or rehabilitation, what was our "doctrine of man"? Was the image of God present in *everyone*? In the face of a psychotic patient suffering from religious hallucinations, was there any sense in which her experiences could be described as a Christian "revelation" (the psychiatrists were busy trying to "cure" her of them)? It was a testing discipline, and not all our students were able to cope with it; but I and my staff believed passionately that it was the right way to prevent a priest, once ordained, from putting away his theological books and continuing on the basis of not much more than common sense (as we saw happening again and again among older clergy). And for me it seemed, and still seems, the validation of my academic study. It brought together the two motivations that had been competing within me, the intellectual and the pastoral. It was as if I had found, and even proved, my vocation.

In addition, I had a gifted and loyal staff. From the start I had insisted that the "chaplain," which was normally the name for the most junior staff member of a theological college, should be a person of wisdom and experience, fit to give spiritual guidance to (mainly young) men in this crucial period of their lives, and I was fortunate that two such sages should have been willing to serve, one a distinguished Cowley Father, Christopher Bryant (the author of some notable books on spirituality and depth psychology), the other a former principal of Pusey House in Oxford, Hugh Maycock, who brought with him not only his own wisdom but also his love of literature and his exceptional gift for sharing that love with others. I treasure one of Hugh's aphorisms. We were discussing maturity. "What is it?" we asked him. His reply was "Seeing the truth of platitudes." On another occasion a high church student went to ask him about some detail of ecclesiastical ritual, knowing him to have presided over a well-known Anglo-Catholic institution. "Ah," said Hugh, "I used to know about such matters, but then I found something else." "What was that, Father?" asked the student, expecting to hear about some still more arcane high church mystery. Hugh's reply was simply, "Religion."

For our children, the move from Oxford had meant a fairly drastic interruption of their education: Marina and Helen were doing well among the few girls at the Dragon School (the boys' preparatory school with which my family had long had a connection). When we moved to Canterbury, Marina was eleven, and her education advanced along conventional lines. Tempted by generous financial terms offered to me as a clergyman, and mesmerized by the head mistress (our first interview had rapidly turned into a stimulating philosophical discussion, quite irrelevant to assessing the suitability of the school), we sent her as a boarder to Benenden. In many ways she flourished there and made at least one good friend (whose parents we quickly identified as being the only ones among all we saw with whom we had anything in common); but we never felt entirely easy with the regime — indeed after leaving Marina there after a holiday (and Helen, who joined her when she was twelve) Julian always felt the need to recover by stopping at Sissinghurst on the way home and regaining some peace of mind from the beauty of the garden. When Marina was sixteen she gained a place as a day girl at the King's School, Canterbury, which had only just begun to take girls in the sixth form. It turned out that the innovation had not been well thought through. The senior boys were already crowded into small studies; and the policy of assigning each girl to one of the studies simply meant she had to choose which boy's knee to sit on. When Marina came home drunk from a party given by one of the assistant masters I lost patience and confronted the headmaster. But he was in his last year and was leaving all reforms to his successor, who in the event was able to ensure that Marina's second year was less fraught. She completed her school years without further mishap; she had also learned to play the clarinet up to quite a high standard (I believe this was mainly to please me: having achieved the top grade she promptly gave it up).

Arrived in Canterbury, Helen and Christian went to a Methodist primary school in the center of the town, where they had to hold their own against some fairly rough children. After a year or two we decided this was not really fulfilling their needs, and sent them to an independent preparatory school. The school was in Deal, fifteen miles away, and we soon realized that this twice-daily journey was ridiculously impractical (even if we could occasionally ask a student to do it for us). After only a term we withdrew them for a spell of informal education at home. It happened that there was a number of elderly retired teachers of considerable talent in Canterbury; one of my students was a former teacher; and I myself took the responsibility for their religious education, which may have been of more benefit to me than to them! I also had to work out a timetable and curriculum that would satisfy the inspectors, a task that I found far more exacting than I expected. By the end it all looked quite good on paper; the reality may have been more like a prolonged holiday for the children. One of the elderly teachers was liable to go to sleep during her lessons, another was prone to illnesses which meant frequent free periods, and lessons in religion were subject to the vagaries caused by my other commitments. But in return the children had far more opportunity for creative occupations such as art and music. They spent many hours in Julian's studio and their freedom from school routine meant we could give them many opportunities for exploring the artistic and historical treasures of East Kent. We also had a resident potter in the college, whom I shall say more about in a moment. He was a brilliant watercolorist as well as a potter, and he generously gave the children much of his time. This has borne fruit in Helen's later life: she now teaches pottery in schools and has established herself as an extremely talented flower painter (she paints under her married name, Helen Simpson). At the ages of twelve and ten the children learned enough during these two years not to feel disadvantaged when they resumed formal education at their secondary schools; and they certainly gained by the stimulus of opportunities that school would never have given them. We felt entirely justified in having made this bold venture in improvised education.

Meanwhile Victoria, when she reached school age, went to a Roman Catholic nuns' school. She had been refused admittance to the state school of our choice because our house lay just outside its catchment area (it was during Margaret Thatcher's time as minister of education and I nearly went to law over what seemed an arbitrarily applied regulation). It was a community apparently unaffected by the Vatican Council except in so far as they were ready to accept an Anglican child; their routine was old-style Catholic, and they had an almost pathological urge to keep checking that small boys and girls were not lurking in pairs behind the bushes. But some learning took place; and Victoria's early life was greatly enriched by a Belgian lady, widow of a British engineer, who lived nearby. She was introduced to us by our parish priest as "someone who might help us." She turned out to be an embodiment of Mary Poppins, endlessly surprising in the pursuits she devised for Victoria — launching her into dancing on the kitchen floor, taking her in the top of a bus to Whitstable, helping her recognize the exotic vegetables she grew in her tiny garden — in short giving her an unexpected bonus of fun and experience almost every time she appeared at our door.

When I took over the college in 1969 I made the unconscious assumption that a course would be appropriate for my students that would have suited the brighter Oxford undergraduates. It soon became apparent that the men from King's, though by no means unintelligent, were simply not prepared to work at the same level of culture. I arranged, for instance, a course on church music on Saturday mornings given by a brilliant church musician. Sydney Evans attended one morning, and said he wished he could be a student again to enjoy that sort of experience; but the students for whom it was designed rapidly dropped off — there was no means of enforcing attendance in the student turmoil of the late sixties — and it had to be abandoned. And the same went for spirituality. I was keen to introduce some of the innovative methods I had seen at Taizé. From the start I organized the students into small "fraternities," and equipped the college with "tiffin carriers" so that each could have a meal together in one of the common rooms — this was how the Taizé monks lived, finding it more stimulating and (in terms of human relationships) more searching and productive of solidarity than sitting down to meals with the whole community; and I tried to reproduce some of its informality and sense of mystery in worship. A few saw the point, but most were apt to snigger. I made a similar experiment with a Cowley Father, who after a spell of missionary work in India, was allowed by his order to start a small house in Sussex for study and practice of Eastern techniques of prayer and meditation. Its effect on my students is well described by Julian.

> Father Slade was an extraordinary man. Tough, small, fearless — and red haired: that meant a temper. He was not to be trifled with! My husband decided that Father Slade was something *needed* for those final-year students ("too cock-sure, too opinionated"). So he — Father Slade — was to come at the beginning of each new year and demonstrate. ("They must put their body into it, gain a wider, more integrated spirituality.") Would they listen, would they appreciate him, I wondered? Could they?
>
> Before chapel time in the old Gateway Chamber he got us going: breathing, slow-walking, our bodies whole so that we should be as one. Several were interested, I realized. But I could see signs of what his red hair might mean! And he was stern, too. Tai Chee had gone well. Now he was at the ultimate stage of Yoga: his feet together, motionless in the air, head below. Here, I knew, he would stay some time. I began to be

nervous and — yes — frightened. Would someone laugh? It would break the whole arc of quiet; more, it might well ruin this new approach to prayer! If anyone sniggered might it not upset him? (He could even fall? — No, I said to myself fiercely). He might be so furious he would never come again. He had so much to give; and "My God," my husband had said, "they need it!"

I dared not look up. Minutes seemed like hours. He was still there, upside down. It would be time for chapel soon. Wasn't that a smirk? A slight guffaw? Not so slight, either. Had he heard? Wouldn't he be irate?

But wasn't that the chapel bell?

Julian was right. He was indeed irate, and I had to spend much of the evening calming down this fiery practitioner of silence and disciplined prayer until he consented to come again; but it was still only a handful of the students who were open enough to benefit from it. A similar result followed from my attempts to persuade them that being an ordained priest had nothing to do with social status, clerical dress or fine vestments (I habitually dressed quite informally myself, and took my turn waiting at table in the dining hall). I had a mature student, a much travelled yachtsman, who had married a French woman. She had been a parishioner of St. Séverin, the church on the Left Bank of the Seine in Paris that was much used by students. The priest, Alain Ponsar, was a wonderfully eloquent and cultivated man, formerly a doctor, who had done much to provide a welcome, through teams of students, to foreign visitors wishing to be guided through some of the most historic churches in France. When he paid a visit to his former parishioner in Canterbury I was able to get to know him, and he remained an intimate friend until his death. He invited me to bring a small group of my ordinands to visit his parish. He was now running a large church further from the center of the city, and was able to arrange for several of his parishioners to welcome the visitors into their homes. On the Saturday evening, when the main mass was celebrated, we experienced the full force of the innovations that a priest with flair and imagination was able to introduce in the wake of the Vatican Council. The church was very large, having been built in the nineteenth century to accommodate pilgrimages from Ste Odile, near Strasbourg. It had numerous side chapels for the priests each to say their own mass (as was customary in those days), and a cavernous nave with rows and rows of seats all facing the distant high altar.

Père Ponsar had drastically altered these arrangements, placing the altar on a platform at the side of the nave and rearranging the seating all round it. He worked with a composer who gathered a group of musicians to accompany the mass with original and engaging music, and the service was conducted with a simplicity and directness that made immediate contact with the very large congregation. We had previously been entertained to a splendid lunch in the presbytery, along with his team of curates and assistants. None wore clerical dress, and much of the conversation was on social issues — the young man next to me, much influenced by Marxism, talked of the need for "perpetual revolution," apparently unaware of the irony of being waited on by a black African girl throughout the meal. All of this amounted to a vivid experience of church life and pastoral activity freed from all the formality and clerical privilege which had been the norm before the Council, and I hoped it would give my students a taste for the same informal and unpretentious style when they returned. To my astonishment and disappointment, they all quietly went off on Sunday morning to the flea market and bought up old vestments which the French clergy had long since abandoned. Evidently the visit had not made the impact that I had hoped, even if none of them was likely to forget it.

More successful, perhaps, was another idea that I had taken from Taizé. There, the presence of an artist and a potter from the beginning had made a considerable contribution to community life. Why should I not have one in the college? By chance I was introduced to a very distinguished potter who was looking for somewhere to live and work. Geoffrey Whiting had been a pupil of Bernard Leach and had developed some designs and glazes of his own of high quality: his teapots were already famous and are now in museums. He was also a superb watercolorist, and we were able to provide space for two exhibitions of his work while he was with us. Though knowing nothing about pottery myself, I was convinced that it would be a wholesome occupation for the students. It is a craft in which one can very soon begin to be creative, and which could be a release for some nervous individuals. And it has the additional virtue that you cannot do it without getting your hands dirty — again, quite a useful experience for young men who were training for what might at times be a ministry in quite earthy circumstances. But Geoffrey's most important contribution was possibly his actual presence in the community as "artist in residence." At this stage of their preparation for ordination, many of the students were prey to much uncertainty about their own fitness for the tasks ahead and the authenticity of their calling. Geoffrey, with his single-mindedness and utter commitment to his craft, was a steadying influence on many — indeed one student actually abandoned thoughts of ordination and became a potter himself, which I thought was probably the right thing for him at that stage: later on he reverted to his original vocation and became an effective priest. Geoffrey also had his influence on us and our family; he gave regular classes to our children, and his beautiful productions in both pottery and painting have adorned our houses ever since. That he was also an occasional alcoholic was just part of the humanity of the artist: in the war against the Japanese he had shot a man without intending to, and this always seemed to haunt his conscience.

In this and many other ways the college was opening up new experiences and new ways of learning for the students. Another valuable element was our fortunate association with a small group of Roman Catholic Franciscans, who joined us almost by chance at the very beginning and remained with us until the end. It happened that two of the Franciscan orders were in the process of starting a training house for their own novices, associated with the new University of Kent at Canterbury. One of these, the Conventuals, had nowhere for their pioneering group to live, and I at once seized the opportunity to have such men sharing our life. One of our buildings was well adapted to giving them their own quarters, and we were able to make one of the two chapels available to them for their services. Not only did this bring an ecumenical dimension into our life, it also gave us the chance to know something of the Franciscan ethos and spirituality at first hand. Father John Jukes was their superior, who later became a bishop, and his total lack of any pomposity, his humor that could defuse most of the personal tensions which he detected around him, and the sheer humanity which shone through him as a monk and a priest, made him an example to the community as well as an immediately trusted friend of our family. One day he was asked by the students whether St. Francis, with his asceticism, his self-inflicted poverty and his simplicity, regarded the things of the world as evil. "No!" he said at once, "the world and everything in it is good. His message is, Move over, and let others enjoy it." I have never heard a better summary of Franciscanism.

But there was one barrier that made it hard for many of the young men to respond in the way I had hoped. This was their own concept of their vocation. Many of them had an image in their minds of the perfect priest, doubtless fashioned from some much older clergyman who had influenced them in their early years, and they strove to protect this image from the currents of change and innovation with which the college was trying to confront them. It was as if they were just battening down the hatches until the storm should have passed, so that after they were safely ordained they could revert to the pattern of ministry that had originally inspired them. Some, indeed, found the challenge altogether too rigorous: it exposed tendencies in them which raised serious questions about their suitability for ordination. On one occasion, after I and the staff had agonized about an individual for many weeks and could send him on to a bishop only with the proviso that we could not honestly recommend him and that he must be very seriously examined before being accepted, our frustration was made almost intolerable by a bishop who, after one short interview, declared that this seemed an admirable candidate and that he did not know what all the fuss was about.

This was just one aspect of the general failure of the church to support what we were doing, even though the methods and in many cases the results were proving their worth and received official approval. There was also the problem of my own character and upbringing. The students' culture was certainly not mine. Not that their social background was necessarily different from that of the undergraduates I had known at Oxford; but instead of the broadening and (dare one say it?) civilizing influence of the Oxford experience they had adapted to a rougher form of social life at King's, where the cultural opportunities were less and the temptation to organize resistance to anything perceived as a threat to their own rights and preferences was much greater. I was of course a stranger to this ethos; and since they had all known each other for three years before coming to Canterbury, the instinct to close ranks against anything that seemed a threat from someone so unlike themselves was very strong. I doubt whether I ever penetrated this barrier with more than a few of them, and I often wondered whether I was the right person for the job. Yet I believed so strongly in what I was trying to do for them that I never seriously thought of abandoning it. The fault, I realized, must lie in myself as much as in them, and it was for me to correct it as best I could.

In fact it lasted only seven years. In 1976 the college was abruptly closed, not because of any serious shortcomings in the training we offered, but in the financial and organizational interests of the church. Finding myself redundant — and receiving a generous redundancy payment from the state, even though, in the event, my next job began the day after I ceased to be warden (we took a family holiday to Gozo on the proceeds) — I applied for a lectureship that was being offered at Oxford and found myself once again in a common room in Christ Church being interviewed by a panel of my former colleagues. The interview developed into a discussion between me and the professor about some abstruse matter of New Testament history until the others lost patience and brought the proceedings to an end. To my surprise I was rung up late that evening to be told I had been appointed.

CHAPTER 6

Consolidation: Oxford Again

Before leaving Canterbury Julian and I had our first experience of church life in the West Indies. I had been invited to attend the meeting of a body called the Anglican Consultative Council, of which the purpose is for representatives of every province worldwide to review matters of pressing concern in the intervals between the ten-yearly Lambeth Conferences. This was to be held in Trinidad, and seemed a good opportunity to accept an invitation I had received some time before to spend a fortnight in Codrington College, Barbados, lecturing to the students preparing for ordination there. In those days Julian and I travelled on separate flights to avoid any risk of leaving the children orphaned, and my flight was a day before hers. When I awoke on my first morning in the principal's house I thought I had never been in such a beautiful place in my life, and sent Julian a telegram to encourage her, trying to describe in a few words the excitement of staying in a Palladian building made of coral with an avenue of palm trees down to a lake with exotic flowers and vividly colored birds. Added to this was the charm and warmth of our hosts. Sehon Goodridge, the principal, was an outstanding Barbadian clergyman, without a trace of the self-indulgent careerism that afflicted many of his fellow clergy. Later he became the first principal of an institute in London for the encouragement and training of black clergy, after which he was summoned back to become bishop of St. Vincent.

At the college he was a genial and imaginative leader, with Janet, his English wife, giving him faithful support and encouragement amidst all the jealousies and intrigues to which the diocese was prone. Their hospitality was exemplary; their only shortcoming was not to have warned us to beware of the other diocesan officials and parish priests who entertained us. Rum was very cheap, and a favorite drink was rum and ginger ale. But the ratio of the one to the other (undetectable once mixed together) was such as to have a serious effect on the sobriety of innocent visitors from Europe. Their students came from all over the Caribbean (apart from Jamaica, which had its own theological college) and were men of widely varied experience and interests; but most of them were endowed with the same uniquely West Indian gift of eloquence. On our last evening, when we were being entertained to dinner in the dining hall, they began to make speeches in our honor with a wit and elegance that none of my own students at Canterbury could have come anywhere near. They then retired to their common room to play dominoes, which they did with such vehemence that the sound of the pieces crashing down on to the table could be heard hundreds of yards away.

In the course of our stay Donald Coggan, then archbishop of Canterbury, made a visit to the island and we attended some of the receptions given for him. He had an extraordinary liking for puns, which seemed to flow out of him spontaneously. After a parish lunch he enquired about the cook and was told that he was (like most professional cooks in the island) Chinese, a Mr. Wong. "Ah," said the archbishop, "Mr. Wong can do no wrong." Shortly before, asking what was in the pudding and being told there were prunes, "Ah yes," he said, "little black workers!" apparently oblivious of the impact this might have on the crowd of uniformly black people who had come to meet him. We then went on to Trinidad together for the conference. The organizer, a somewhat austere man, had decreed that none of the delegates should bring their wives: he had been outraged at the previous meeting in Dublin, when delegates tended to go off shopping with their spouses instead of attending the sessions. The Coggans, assuming the privilege of status, ignored the ruling and were grudgingly accommodated together. But Julian was an altogether different case. When we arrived at the former American air base, far from the capital, where the conference was to be held, she was rapidly expelled

84

and sent to stay with the local bishop, a portentous man named Abdullah, and his gracious Japanese wife.

While the meetings were in progress Mrs. Coggan paid visits to schools and hospitals on the island, and suggested that Julian should accompany her. She was a charming and generous person, who had given up a medical career to marry the future archbishop. (Her maiden name was Strain: "Can the Cog take the Strain?" had been the chant of Donald's students, knowing his fascination with puns.) She also had a strong evangelical faith, and did not hesitate to talk to the children about the Lord Jesus even though the majority were Muslims or Hindus. Thus Julian found both pleasure and occasional embarrassment in her role as unofficial lady-in-waiting to the archbishop's wife; on Mrs. Coggan's side there was a corresponding oscillation between appreciation of Julian's charming and vivacious company and surprise at her spontaneity and acute observation. "What strange things you notice, Mrs. Harvey," she said on one occasion. As for my own part in the conference, I was assigned to a section preparing a report on a particular aspect of the church's ministry, and found myself with a dual role. My brief was to be a "theological consultant." In practice I became the scribe who drafted the report (there being no other member of the section prepared to take it on), but I also had the task of restraining the chairman, an Australian archbishop, who was determined we should rush through our work at maximum speed so that he could escape to watch the test match that was in progress in Port of Spain.

We returned to England in time for the last term of the college's existence and performed its obsequies with a dinner prepared by one of my students (who had been a professional chef) and attended by surviving members of the previous regimes — the Central College and the Missionary College that preceded it — who came for this somewhat emotional occasion from as far afield as Ottawa and Tokyo. We then returned to our house in Oxford, which had been let to tenants during the last seven years, though I left Julian with two of our daughters in one of the small college cottages in Canterbury for a further term for the sake of the children's education, and in order to make our bitterly cold house more welcoming for the family. Once again, not content with the purely academic college fellowship and university lectureship to which I had been appointed, I rashly took on in addition the chaplaincy of another college. Thus I found myself with considerably more than a full-time job, in which a genuine professionalism on either the academic or the pastoral side was bound to suffer.

In six years I achieved what would today be regarded as a bare minimum of publications, and my activities as college chaplain were at times fairly perfunctory. Not that it wasn't hugely enjoyable and stimulating. I was a full member of two colleges, one (Wolfson) a large graduate society embracing a wide range of different specialisms, the other (Queens') an ancient foundation primarily concerned with the education of undergraduates in core university subjects. The contrast was exhilarating and exposed me to many challenges, both intellectual and personal. At The Queens' College, where I was chaplain, I rapidly learned to respect the pastoral gifts and conscientiousness of many of the tutors and was able confidently to leave much of the care of undergraduates to them, concentrating more on stimulating interest in the larger questions of ethics, religion, and spirituality. At Wolfson, where I was a fellow, though there were colleagues whose work was related to mine, I was frequently made to realize how foreign my own subject must seem to experts in such things as forestry, radiology, sinology, or nuclear physics. One day I found myself sitting next to a scientist who asked me about my subject. "Theology," I said, which he misheard as "geology" and had to be helped to understand what I was talking about. I then explained that I worked primarily on the New Testament. "Rather a small book, isn't it, on which to spend so much time?" After that bracing comment I resolved never to become a specialist *within* the discipline: there could be no justification for devoting myself exclusively (as some do) to the study of just a part of the subject — Jesus, Paul, textual criticism, and the like. Surely he was right. The small book called the New Testament, despite the immense complexity of its history and interpretation, should not be too much for one person to tackle with academic rigor.

Apart from my academic work in the university and from cultivating the social contacts and research opportunities offered by my two colleges, there was plenty to do in the chaplaincy and the chapel

at Queens'. There was a strong musical tradition and an excellent undergraduate choir, as well as the long-established Eglesfield Music
Society (named after the co-founder of the college) directed by the
music fellow and organist, James Dalton. James had been a contemporary of mine as an undergraduate at Worcester College, and it was
he who suggested that I should become the chaplain. It was a partnership I much enjoyed, and resulted in some exceptionally beautiful
acts of worship. James had prevailed on a reluctant Governing Body
to replace the dilapidated organ he had inherited with one of the first
and finest baroque organs to be built in England after the war. The
result was a magnificent instrument built by Frobenius, a Danish
organ builder, which attracted distinguished players from all over the
world to give recitals. James himself performed on that instrument
the entire organ works of Bach in the course of one year, and drew a
large and appreciative audience.

The other fellows, however, kept their distance from the chapel.
In Queens' there was a long tradition, if not of anticlericalism, then
at least of deliberate indifference. "This is a place of piety and learning," they had been reminded by a former provost, himself in Holy
Orders. "Yes, provost," they are reputed to have replied, "we will take
care of the learning but will leave the piety to you." Not that I experienced any personal animosity; but virtually none of them attended
any chapel service, even when Stuart Blanch, the archbishop of York
who was also the Visitor of the College, came to preach at one Sunday
Evensong (they said to me afterwards, "Would you really have preferred us to commit the hypocrisy of attending just for that reason?").
The provost, on the other hand, was a regular attender. Robert Blake,
by now Lord Blake, had been a history don at Christ Church during
my time there and had subsequently moved to Queens' as provost.
He and his family became intimate friends, and he gave me firm and
loyal support all the time I was there. He was an archetypal lay member of the Church of England, faithfully supporting its traditions and
convinced of the value of its contribution to national life. He certainly rested his own ethical integrity firmly on the basis of Christian
teaching, but without any apparent interest in the deeper matters of
personal religion. One day I brought in to dinner a wise priest who

was to give a talk on spirituality in chapel later in the evening. When the provost asked him what he was going to talk about, he replied, "I am going to try to help them use their solitude." "Ah yes," said the provost, "I don't think that is something I would be very good at."

The university lectureship involved teaching, lecturing, examining, and occasionally interviewing candidates for admission to the colleges with which I was associated, as well as some routine administrative tasks. In addition there was the expectation that I would make a significant contribution to scholarship in my field. Whether I succeeded in doing so must be for others to judge (though I certainly received some commendation). But I also felt that I stood a little apart from the methods and interests of most of my colleagues. I can relate this to developments I had observed in my subject during the second half of the twentieth century. The great innovations in New Testament scholarship associated with Martin Dibelius, Rudolf Bultmann, and others, which involved dismembering the texts into small units and tracing their assumed origin in independent traditions, were greatly enlivened by the breadth of learning of these (mainly German) scholars. Having received the benefit of a traditional German education, they were good classical scholars as well as theologians; and they were also expert in and deeply influenced by the great German philosophers of the late nineteenth and early twentieth centuries. But their successors, whose education had much less of the traditional foundation in the classics and philosophy, made use of the same critical methods but without the same enlivening background. I wrote an article in the seventies entitled "Is New Testament Study Still Interesting?" in which I drew attention to the diminishing returns of the fashionable critical techniques, the poverty of new information being offered, and the risk of the subject becoming of little interest to any but narrow specialists. By contrast, I welcomed the arrival on the scene of interested scholars from other disciplines — literary criticism, sociology, linguistics — which had brought a breath of fresh air to the theology departments of some American faculties. For my own part I felt a particular sympathy for these new approaches in that my career had involved a much deeper acquaintance with the worlds of Greece and Rome than was possessed by most of my fellow practitioners, and moreover I had made my way in the guild of New Testament scholars without ever having had the formal schooling that was normally demanded. Consequently I felt a kinship with those who had made what was still an unconventional entry into the subject, and went so far as to publish a collection of essays that I entitled "Alternative Approaches to New Testament Study" — not an exact title, since some of the contributors were doing fairly conventional work. But all had come to it by paths other than the usual ones, and most of them brought gifts and interests which promised to refresh the staleness into which I felt the subject was falling. Some were grateful also for a champion who could help to make their work known and establish their acceptability.

One of these was a scholar of astonishing breadth of learning whom I had met during my previous spell at Oxford. I had been working on St. John's Gospel for my *Companion* and was perplexed by the way in which at one point Jesus insists on the requirement for two witnesses to vouch for him, but later seems content with only one. None of the commentaries were any help; but I had read articles by a certain J. Duncan M. Derrett, which seemed to show an expert knowledge of the intricacies of ancient Jewish legal procedure. The immense learning and massively dense footnotes with which his opinions were supported led me to imagine him as an elderly polymath with a shock of white hair and a thick guttural accent denoting a cosmopolitan education somewhere in continental Europe. Who was I to address a simple technical question to such a formidable authority? However I summoned up courage to write him a letter, and, hearing nothing for some time, was ready to assume that he would hardly attend to problems addressed to him by such small fry as myself. Then, a few weeks later, there was a knock on the door of my rooms in Christ Church and in walked a youngish man, sleek and neat in appearance, who sat down on my sofa with a patter of conversation about the way Oxford colleges never had their name written on the gate, and then announced, "By the way, my name is Derrett." I could not have been more surprised.

This was the beginning of a long association which developed into a close friendship. I had not been mistaken about the extent of his learning. He had, like me, studied Greek and Latin at Oxford; then, during a spell with the army in India, he had learnt Sanskrit and become a passionate student of Hinduism. He then studied law, and gained a position at the London School of African and Oriental Studies to teach Indian law. Feeling a need to broaden his interests, he turned to Hebrew law, rapidly learning Hebrew for the purpose, while developing his expertise in comparative law and comparative religion. He then accompanied his wife to church one day and heard the notoriously puzzling parable of the Unjust Steward. Believing that he knew the answer to its conundrums, he read up the massive secondary literature in a few weeks and published an article in a New Testament journal which came to the notice of the panel of scholars who were working on the *New English Bible* and caused them to revise their translation in accordance with his conclusions. Thereafter, New Testament studies became one of his main interests (along with Sanskrit Buddhist texts, in which he also made himself expert) and he went on to publish a spate of books and articles which brought his legal intuitions and sharply critical intelligence to bear on many questions which had puzzled the professionals for years, often yielding new solutions. But he also became convinced (and here he was generally at fault) that the professionals felt threatened by what he was offering and were doing their best to ignore him or even discredit him. I felt it was a necessary service both to him and to my colleagues to support him and help to get his work accepted as an invaluable contribution to our research. His publications did soon begin to make their way; but his abiding sense of being rejected remained, and my efforts to disabuse him, which went on to the end of his life, were never entirely successful.

By adding to all this a college chaplaincy I virtually forfeited my leisure time, and had to leave to Julian most of the care of the home and family. True, this was now less onerous. Marina was away at university, first in London and then in Bangor, where her degree in marine biology enabled her to go on to obtain an MSc in aquaculture and fisheries in Stirling; Helen, by now sixteen, was still a boarder at Benenden until she joined us in Oxford to prepare for Oxford entrance exams. Having been unsuccessful in these, she spent some months teaching crafts to patients in a large hospital in India, an experience which convinced her that she should become an artist. As a result she did a foundation course in Banbury and was then accepted for an undergraduate course in fine arts at the Royal Academy Schools in London. Christian, when we left Canterbury, had been doing well at the Simon Langton (which was in the process of being transformed from a grammar school to a comprehensive), and was particularly enjoying the teaching she received there in classics; and after just a week or two of a school we chose for her near Oxford she firmly applied to be readmitted in Canterbury and herself arranged to be a lodger with one of our friends, even though this meant cycling into town each day through the orchards; and this continued until she joined the sixth form at the Girls' High School in Oxford, from which she gained a place at Worcester College. Consequently, for much of the time, Victoria was the only one of our children living at home. Like two of her sisters she went to the Dragon School, and stayed there till she was thirteen. It was, she said later, the best education she had anywhere. It gave her also a grounding in the classics such that the high school, to which she proceeded, was not able to take her forward within her age group, and it was fortunate that it was only a year later that we moved to London and were able to arrange schooling more appropriate to her needs.

Meanwhile Julian had more chance to paint and to write, attending art classes and a poetry group and even a course leading to a G.C.E. in Italian. Since I was often required to be in college in the evenings my own appearances at home were almost limited to Saturday afternoons and a blessed interval on Sundays between the morning service and College Evensong — except of course in vacations when I tried to make up for my dereliction of family duties by spending much more time at home and making family holidays a priority each summer. She was thus much on her own; and the loneliness she felt at times must often have been compounded by problems with her stepmother. When Ian returned from Florence in 1958, after Jane had died, he was appointed by the Bishop of Sheffield (Leslie Hunter) as warden of the newly established diocesan retreat and conference house, Whirlow Grange, almost on the edge of the Peak District. His youthful ambitions — to be a diplomat or a priest like his father — had been stymied by the attack of poliomyelitis which had disabled him early in his time at The King's School Canterbury and was at that period a disqualification for either profession; but one part of them had been unexpectedly fulfilled when he found himself consul in Florence, the other was now partially satisfied in a post which enabled him to use his considerable pastoral gifts with the many and varied church people who came to Whirlow Grange. This lasted a few years and gave him great satisfaction. It was a period of experimentation in church ministry, and Sheffield was the center of a new venture in industrial mission. The priests who conducted this would make a point of removing their collars and mixing with working people in pubs and canteens: this (they naively believed) would help to break down barriers between the church and the world of work. It was Ian, with his unerring intuition and sensitivity, who quietly engaged with those who came to Whirlow Grange and tactfully informed the missioners that a number of those whom they believed they had attracted to the Christian religion by their innovative approach had in fact for some years been church wardens in their parish churches.

This period came to an end after a few years, when Mary Neville, a physiotherapist and former friend of Jane's, paid a surprise visit to Whirlow Grange and persuaded Ian to marry her. She was an exceedingly determined lady, whose powers of persuasion had enabled her to start a nursing home in Oxford which she hoped would be a half-way house between hospital and normal life for orthopedic patients, on whom she could exercise her professional skills. In the event the majority of those who applied for rooms were elderly people requiring care for the infirmities of old age, and her original dream of restoring youthful bodies to their physical prime was never fulfilled. But the nursing home prospered, thanks to her extraordinary success in raising the necessary funds. That same gift of determination secured Ian as her husband, and the marriage took place in Christ Church Cathedral during my time there. But the marriage was not without its difficulties, especially for Julian (to Ian's distress). At one stage Mary resorted to a medium and learned from friends on the Other Side that Julian was evil and that Ian must be protected from her; and indeed there was one occasion when she threatened Julian with one of Ian's crutches in full view of his small grandchildren, who adored him. The times that we were able to have Ian staying with us on family holidays (which gave him intense delight) were always the result of long and fraught negotiations. Finally, at the end of his life (he died in 1978), Ian was lodged in the nursing home, and it was observed that Mary seemed to treat him as a patient rather than as a husband: she would go back home at five o'clock as she always had, leaving Ian in the care of her staff. But this was Julian's opportunity. She would creep unobserved into Ian's room quite late at night and spend hours with him, accompanying him on his journey towards death and repairing the sense of separation which his second marriage had induced. It was an experience that she found deeply enriching; but the sense of loss that followed his death was hard for her to bear. She gave it expression in one of the poems she wrote soon after for the poetry workshop of which she was a member:

> Lord, too much death has made me dull —
> That stiffening of a much-loved face.
> On poet's listening falls a lull;
> I only walk at funeral pace.
>
> The horrid absence of a soul
> Curbs my rare freedom, my free will;
> A tenantless body takes control,
> Medusa-like it casts its spell.
>
> This soul, too precious to disappear,
> Seems oddly to have left no trace.
> Such emptiness fills me with fear:
> How to resume my normal pace?

This may well have been one of the factors which brought on the crisis that was soon to follow. 1980 had been a singularly successful year for me in academic terms. In 1979 I had been elected to give the prestigious Bampton lectures the following year. I persuaded Sehon

Goodridge, who was still in Barbados, to take a sabbatical and replace me in Queens' for a term so that I could have a sabbatical myself for working on the lectures. The arrival of this black clergyman caused something of a sensation in the college, but his charm and abilities soon made him so popular that he was allowed to stay on as my assistant for two more terms. He entered fully into college life, even joining us for the Commemoration Ball at the end of the summer where, bathed in perspiration and dressed in an ill-fitting dinner jacket I had lent him, he went back and forth from the table at which we, as spectators rather than as dancers, were decorously passing the evening, saying with characteristic enthusiasm, "Boy, I love dancing!"

My Bampton lectures, given as sermons on successive Sunday mornings in the University Church, attracted a faithful audience (which included our youngest daughter Victoria, aged twelve, who was seen every time in the front row, listening with apparently rapt attention) and were later published. In the same summer I learned that I had won a prize for a poem submitted to a competition open to all graduates of the university for a "Poem on a Sacred Subject." The subject prescribed was "Thou hast appealed unto Caesar; unto Caesar shalt thou go." It was Julian who was first attracted by the idea of entering, but, not seeing how to tackle it, she consulted me, with the result that I became interested and (with her ready consent) also competed myself. I submitted about a hundred lines of blank verse in the form of a reflective monologue uttered by the Roman official who was handling Paul's case, and to my great surprise was awarded the prize, which obliged me to circulate the poem to all heads of colleges and divinity professors but also, to my astonishment, carried a financial reward sufficient to take Julian and two of our daughters to Greece for a fortnight.

It was during that otherwise enchanted stay in the British Archaeological School in Athens (the students being on vacation we were generously offered rooms) that we first became seriously alarmed by Julian's times of depression. We had been aware for some time that all was not well with her, but had taken the natural course of hoping and expecting that she would pull out of it. But her moments of misery, amid and despite the stimulating surroundings of Greece, were more alarming; and later that year they developed into a major breakdown which required long spells in the very hospital of which I had been chaplain fifteen years before. Not that this made things easier: the regime had changed out of recognition, the psychiatric fashion now being to treat patients only in groups, the staff on principle making themselves inaccessible and confining their attention to the correct administration of drugs. And not only drugs. The consultants insisted that her life would be in danger (literally, so the doctrine went at the time) if she was not given ECT (ElectroConvulsive Therapy), and I was unable to prevent her being subjected to two courses, one apparently successful, but only briefly, the other continuing for several weeks and yielding no improvement at all (and who knows with what sinister consequences for her mind and memory in the future?). The inhumanity of the treatment and the distortion of her personality — and even of her physical appearance — which accompanied it were a searing experience. I remember coming out of the hospital and sitting in the car, pulling down my hat to conceal my tears. Gradually there was improvement, and Julian was discharged, only to be re-admitted a few weeks later; and the illness continued on and off for three years, including two short spells in hospital after we had moved to London. If it was agony for me, what must it have been like for her? A poem she wrote soon after gives us a glimpse.

Two years I lost, two crowded precious years.
As some poor butterfly, when winter comes,
Loses the scent of nectar-giving flowers,
And lingers, un-nourished, feeling only fears.
I, muddled, purposeless, flew here and there,
Suspicious of the one who shared my life,
Afraid of how my children's lives could go,
Without direction, exile everywhere.
Through salt tears I dug nails into my palms
And laid my head against the bolted doors.
They gave me massive ministry of drugs —
Unrelated, a number in a file —
Where problem-solving doctor, nurse (and char!)

With their blunt tools laid bare the patient's mind.
Behind glass doors the doctors sat and talked,
The waiting patients vainly sought a glance....

Characteristically, she remained sensitively aware of others and felt deeply for them even amid her own confusion. She wrote of one of them, "Sarah,"

She made us think of Reynolds's Tragic Muse,
Her features static, her walk somnambulant.
Her husband's formal visit done, she'd stand
Till sweat like lichen flowers formed on her brow.
Mouth plummeting, soul trapped, her voice would ask,
'Am I mad?'
We too were threatened by her fear, and paused:
'No, Sarah, you're not mad.'
'Yes,' she said (not hearing) 'I'll be good,
I'll wash my hair, I'll do the crossword....'
I think we hated the banality
The emptiness where something fine had been,
Where eyes had had a beauty and a depth.
'Can't you do something for her?' we would ask.
Their answer always was, 'She's better now.'
'Better!' — strutting, pill-taking human form!
'Freed,' they firmly said, 'from her obsessions' —
Severed from contemplation....

During this time the older children had already begun their adult lives away from home, and Victoria, still at the Dragon School in Oxford, became my main support and helped me through this, the most difficult time in my life — at a cost to her own emotional development, which we were only to realize years later.

Yet despite this, these years are ones that I look back on with gratitude. In the late seventies Oxford was a wonderful place to be. The following decades were to see the introduction of a more rigorous regime for academic staff, with relentless pressure to publish, and independent monitoring of individual performance in lecturing, teaching, and research. But in the seventies we were still relatively free to work out the best use of our own time, and we could still, if we wished, follow our better instincts and give absolute priority to the needs of our pupils, in partnership (not competition) with our colleagues. In my chaplaincy work, I found that the students had lost the angry restiveness of the sixties and had become, indeed, dismayingly timid and conservative — I sometimes felt I was the only radical in the room when I entertained them. But they were also open and trusting, and a number of them became lasting friends of me and my family. As for my colleagues, they had been more disposed to treat me with consideration than when I was in my thirties at Christ Church, and both my new colleges had relaxed the strict exclusiveness of former days and gave a welcome to Julian on many occasions, so that she felt much less isolated from the world in which I spent most of my time than had been the case fifteen years or so before. It was also a time of invigorating change at Oxford. Men's colleges were at last opening their doors to female undergraduates, who brought a new and welcome flavor to college life. They also created a change in the rhythm of my tutorials. I found I now needed a box of Kleenex handkerchiefs in my cupboard to cope with the moments when a girl would suddenly dissolve into tears — not usually because she was in such awe of me, but more often because she had had an emotional upset with a boyfriend the night before.

In my own academic work I also felt a stronger sense of direction. My *Companion to the New Testament*, written twenty years before, was by now well established and eventually sold some forty thousand copies. The book was seen as relatively conservative with regard to modern critical opinions — I was convinced, for instance, of the general veracity of the gospels, even if many details of their narratives may have been embroidered or even invented over time. Any originality possessed by my commentary I put down to the influence of my father. He had died several years before I completed it, but his brilliant legal mind and consistent agnosticism had unconsciously trained me to ask questions of the text that tended to be ignored or evaded in the standard commentaries. This questioning, along with the distinctive approach of one who had come to the New Testament as a classical scholar rather than as a well-trained theologian, set me somewhat apart from the established "guild" of New Testament scholars. Indeed I remained skeptical of many of the alleged advances of scholarship, and frequently warned my students not to trust the too-confident statements they would find in the standard textbooks. After all, I told them, most of what I and my colleagues were teaching them was supposition; there was very little that we actually *knew* that they could not have inferred themselves from the biblical text. True, there are not many certainties that we can distill from the gospels; but I am convinced there are some, and I made them the subject of my Bampton Lectures, which were published under the title *Jesus and the Constraints of History* in 1982. In the lectures I had tried to anchor certain moments in the story of Jesus through historical research into the circumstances and culture in which he lived. I had chosen this theme since understanding Jesus must always be the most important area of New Testament study and the one most relevant to faith and discipleship. To this extent my academic work at this stage was consistent with my concern for its application to daily living.

In sum, I was gaining the reputation of a conscientious and competent university teacher and moderately successful chaplain. I had not seriously neglected any of the three ways — ministry, profession, marriage — which I had always felt drawn to follow. But the old uncertainties remained. Was I really destined to work in universities all my life? By being over-extended with too many occupations (membership of the C. of E. Doctrine Commission was added to the list, for which I wrote substantial contributions), was I not simply entrenching a certain amateurishness which should disqualify me (if I was honest) from a senior post? In the event, the decision was taken out of my hands. Julian was now suffering from periods of depression (they continued for the next twenty-five years), and it became impossible to manage my work in Oxford from our house two miles from the center when I could be called on at any time to cope with her needs. When a letter arrived from the prime minister inviting me to be canon theologian of Westminster there was really no question that I ought to accept.

CHAPTER 7

Application: Westminster

C anon of Westminster. Here was a job I could do from home, caring intensively for Julian when need arose; and I could be persuaded that it was an opportunity, like the Canterbury experience, for bringing my intellectual understanding of the Christian faith to bear on public issues and pastoral tasks. Certainly it gave me time for some strictly academic work, even though my colleagues were not always convinced I was spending it appropriately: I had to struggle to persuade them that after seven years I should be granted a short sabbatical — just long enough to do a term's part-time teaching at Berkeley, California, in one of the theological colleges on "holy hill," and to do the research for a new book (this time on Christian ethics) in their amazingly well-stocked and well-serviced theological library. Julian was with me, and we were given the visiting professor's flat overlooking the palm trees and dignified buildings of the campus — which inspired her to do several striking paintings — and we both enjoyed the warmth of American hospitality and the chance to visit the natural wonders of the great Redwood forests and the valleys and waterfalls of Yosemite.

As the one member of the Abbey staff who had solid academic experience I was entrusted with a range of tasks, such as initiating, finding funding for, and supervising the refurbishment of the Abbey museum with its unique collection of funeral effigies of kings and queens of England, overseeing the library, revising the statutes, and masterminding the important and (at the time) exceedingly exciting

project of erecting ten statues of twentieth century Christian martyrs on the west front of the Abbey. All of this went along with offering a great deal of hospitality in our large and commodious house in
the precincts, regular attendance at and occasionally creative contributions to the Abbey worship, and frequent contact and collaboration with a wide range of people, some of them holding great national
responsibilities. It was a full, stimulating, and satisfying ministry, and
gave opportunity for many of my alleged "gifts" to come into play.
And at the same time I was continuing to write books, articles, and
reviews that claimed attention from my former academic colleagues.
I realized that I was continuing to enjoy their respect (though some
remained puzzled by the course I had chosen, and sought to persuade
me to return to Oxford); and yet a slight sense of amateurishness
remained. Was my reputation really well founded? Had I simply got
by, keeping my ventures severely within the limits I could cope with
and bluffing my way out when cornered?

But life at the Abbey was far too full and eventful for such doubts
to be much in my mind. When I arrived in 1982 Edward Carpenter,
having been a canon for many years (and passed over for higher office as too liberal and unorthodox until Harold Wilson made him
dean) was still in the deanery and remained there for my first three
years. I had known him for some time (one of his greatest friends
was François Piachaud, my vicar when I was a curate twenty years
before) and I had long had the greatest admiration, not just for his
intellectual brilliance — he was a first-rate philosopher and historian
— but for his engaging and unusual informality both in private conversations and on formal public occasions. One could call at the deanery at any time of day, and would be welcomed without the smallest
indication that one was interrupting anything more important. Late
at night he would mount his bicycle and ride around London, and
then settle down to serious historical work until the early hours of
the morning (at the time he was writing his massive biography of
Archbishop Geoffrey Fisher). He and his wife Lilian, equally surprising and unconventional (she was reputed to have welcomed callers
while standing on her head doing yoga, and was known to follow
the Baha'i faith at least as enthusiastically as Christianity), created

a sense of informal ease and accessibility that permeated the whole Abbey community. Indeed Edward had an exceptional ability to engage with people of every kind. I tried to express this in the sermon I was invited to preach at his funeral in 1998:

> The past, for him (as with all passionate historians), was never in a category of its own, something to be considered apart from the present and the future. It furnished him, not just with material for study, but with friends and partners — thinkers, poets, statesmen — with whom he could maintain a constant dialogue as he painstakingly built up his own store of practical wisdom and experience. When Shelley or Byron or one of the First World War poets (whose monument in Poets' Corner was one of his most cherished achievements) cropped up in his talk, as they so often did, they were not there just for embroidery or illustration; they were participants in the endlessly questing conversation taking place in his mind and which he had a unique gift of sharing with others   with prince or tradesman, introverted intellectual or uncomplicated supporter of Chelsea Football Club, indeed with anyone who crossed his path or, as often, encountered him on his bicycle, in such a way that each of us seemed to have been caught up in his own personal dialogue with the great thinkers — and sometimes sportsmen — of the past, and yet (perhaps because of his unfailing humour and courtesy) were made to feel perfectly at ease in that unexpected and, for some of us, unfamiliar company.

He was a fluent and arresting preacher as well as an acute political and religious commentator and controversialist, and conversation with him always held some surprises. The thought of working at close quarters with him was certainly one of the factors which persuaded me to accept the canonry when it was offered to me, and I had an early experience of it when he initiated the Abbey's response to the massacre of Palestinians at Chatila in Lebanon in the autumn of 1982. It happened that the other canons were all away, and it fell to

me to assist him in any way I could to fashion an event that would
help people to come to terms with the catastrophe. Edward had
conceived the idea of an hour's silent prayer in the nave attended
by the leaders of all three faiths — Judaism, Islam, and Christianity
— punctuated only by an occasional prayer said by a representative
of each faith in turn. But he knew that simply issuing the invitation
would hardly be enough to fill a space that holds nearly a thousand
people; so he spent an entire day on the phone successfully cajoling
everyone he could think of, from bishops, senior rabbis, and imams
to politicians and community leaders, both to attend themselves and
to persuade others to do so. The result was a full congregation for
whom an hour's shared silent prayer was exactly the right means of
defusing the immediate violent anger that was felt by so many and
turning their minds toward positive opportunities for forgiveness,
reparation, and reconciliation.

Equally characteristic of Edward was his reaction when Mrs.
Thatcher, who was in Brussels, surprised everyone by announcing,
without consultation, that there would be a service to commemorate
the fortieth anniversary of VE day in Westminster Abbey. She further stipulated that this would be for British people only: apart from
the corps diplomatique no foreigners would be invited. In effect, she
wanted an old-fashioned victory service. This proposal Edward ada-
mantly refused to accept (the press instantly reviled him as a pacifist,
which indeed he was by conviction, but this had nothing to do with
the present case). He obtained the support of other church leaders
and began serious negotiation with the government. Yes, he argued,
by all means let there be a service to mark the anniversary of the
end of the war in Europe; but after forty years such a service should
surely not be held unless there were representatives present of all the
nations involved, the vanquished alongside the victors. After much
argument the concession was granted, but on one condition: only a
church representative from each country could be invited — and the
Abbey would have to pay their expenses! We immediately mobilized
all those living within the precincts to give hospitality to these distinguished guests — all except the Russians, who sent two prelates and
the inevitable interpreter/government informer, none of whom was

permitted to stay in a private house. The Abbey found itself having to bear the cost of lodging them in a nearby hotel, for which they duly presented a bill so high that we assumed it could only have been the result of lavish expenditure on telephone calls to Moscow and vodka.

But the service fully repaid our trouble. Its most moving and impressive moment was when a church leader from each of the nations walked up the length of the Abbey alongside his counterpart from a former enemy country. All were then greeted by the archbishop of Canterbury before the high altar and solemnly exchanged the peace with him and with one another. What had been envisaged, independently of us, as a nationalistic celebration of victory was transformed by Edward into an occasion for mutual recognition and reconciliation. In doing so he was bravely following a precedent that had been set only three years before in St. Paul's Cathedral by Robert Runcie, then archbishop of Canterbury, when the end of the Falklands war was commemorated by a service that included prayers for the Argentinians and the Lord's Prayer in Spanish. Once again Mrs. Thatcher was denied her victory service, now with strong popular support.

That event was the first of a long series of occasions when we had the joy and privilege of entertaining in our house an amazing variety of memorable people. The church leader allotted to us came from East Berlin. He surprised us by arriving two days before we were expecting him, for the good reason that he had at last received his visa from the East German authorities and did not dare delay using it in case it was withdrawn before he travelled (such things often happened). Werner Krätschel was a Lutheran pastor whose parish in Berlin actually included the Stasi headquarters. His visit gave him the opportunity, otherwise denied to an East German, to meet his opposite number from West Berlin, who was staying with my colleague next door; but it also began a friendship with him and his wife (whom we met later) and bore fruit a few years later in a visit I made with the Abbey choir to his large parish church.

Also in Edward Carpenter's time we had the privilege of meeting the Dalai Lama. Fear of the Chinese reaction had made both the government and the royal family unwilling to receive him when he

visited London in 1984; but Edward bravely defied all official disapproval (and not a little dismay among the Abbey community) and
invited this officially unwelcome visitor to stay at the deanery. The
disruption this caused for him and his activities as dean were such
as few other church dignitaries would have contemplated enduring;
but Edward somehow worked through and around the revolution
that the Dalai Lama and his staff caused in the deanery. He and Lilian turned out of their bedroom, which was totally reorganized and
refurnished so as to have the bed pointing in the required direction
and all pictures and ornaments removed to make room for his own
sacred objects and style of decoration; monks slept on the stairs as
bodyguards, all his food was tasted before he ate it, and the kitchen
was entirely taken over for his needs. Lilian, undeterred, discovered
that his birthday would occur during his stay, and arranged a family
party for him. A birthday cake was made in accordance with his di-
etary rules, candles were lighted, and he was persuaded to take the
knife and cut the first slice — something that he had probably never
done since he was a child, since all such domestic things were done by
others for him. We then all sang Happy Birthday, and, after a moment
of astonishment, he was clearly delighted. It was difficult to resist the
humor, the gentleness, and the sheer humanity of the man who had
spent most of his life in exile, carrying the burdens of his oppressed
and persecuted people. For our own part, we gave hospitality to two
of his staff, one of whom was the minister for home affairs of the
government-in-exile. Their visit gave us a privileged moment of insight into the gifts and trials of Tibetans and into the extraordinarily
impressive character of the Dalai Lama himself.

Less personal, but also impressive, were some of the formal visits
paid by heads of state to lay a wreath at the grave of the Unknown
Warrior. Mikhail Gorbachev came in 1989, and after the wreath laying, when we normally had a prayer for peace and reconciliation, we
asked him, as head of an officially atheist state, whether we might
do so on this occasion. He assented at once, and made sure that the
interpreter was next to him so that he should catch the words accu-
rately. He then turned to Mrs. Thatcher (it was unusual for the prime
minister to attend, but she clearly thought this was an exceptional

occasion), and, after making sure that the press was listening, said to her, "That prayer was the agenda for our talks, was it not?" By contrast, Boris Yeltsin, who came a few years later, laid his wreath, gazed at the grave and, looking red in the face, growled out (in English), "This must never happen again!" It was not long after this that he authorized a brutal military campaign in Chechnya.

The Japanese emperor and empress also impressed us. Their visit in 1998 had been preceded by a flurry of protest and agitation. On the one hand, the Burma Star, an association of those who had suffered imprisonment in Japanese camps during the war, were determined that the emperor should be made aware of the bitterness they felt over their treatment as P.O.Ws and of their demand for reparation, and had organized protests along the route he would follow. On the other, an association called the Burma Campaign Fellowship Group, composed also of former P.O.Ws in Japanese camps, were committed to reconciliation and friendship with the rising Japanese generation, and had campaigned for giving the emperor a warm reception. They found that both H.M. Government and Buckingham Palace were on their side, and their senior members were duly rewarded by the privilege of a seat at the banquet given by the queen during the state visit. Their secretary had called on me some weeks before to make sure that the Abbey shared their views, and I responded by proposing that we might make rather more of the formal wreath-laying visit than usual. I suggested that the dean might make a short speech of welcome, issued to the press, that would make it absolutely clear that we disassociated ourselves completely from the people who would be booing the emperor outside. I then drafted a speech for the dean to deliver.

Meanwhile my friend from the fellowship group had informed the Japanese embassy of our proposal, where it caused agitation and dismay. "But the emperor," they said, "is above all political issues. We cannot have anyone saying things publicly about him that might seem controversial." They even sent a senior diplomat around to persuade me to give up the idea. However I was able to reassure him that the proposed address would have no serious implications for the emperor, and that the ambassador could see a draft and ask for amendments if he wished; and finally we received approval. When the emperor and empress came to the Abbey, rather more had been arranged for them than usual. A group had been gathered of around twenty grandchildren of those who had been interned in the Japanese camps, and the duke of Edinburgh, who had commanded one of the ships that brought them home, was also in attendance. After the formal ceremony the emperor and empress were invited to meet the young people; and we were amazed by the ease and informality with which they talked with them, considerably over-running their schedule and evidently much enjoying the experience. Living as they do in relative isolation even from their own people, to have shown such assurance talking to a younger generation in a language not their own, with Prince Philip occasionally chipping in with his own recollections, struck us as a remarkable display of character, and one that fully justified all that we had done to make something memorable of their visit.

Most impressive of all, perhaps, was the state visit of Nelson Mandela in 1996. When he entered the Abbey, we were standing as usual in a line to greet him and shake his hand one by one. When he reached me I said the obvious thing about being glad to welcome him, to which he replied, looking me straight in the face, "But it is a privilege to meet you." From anyone else this would have been a rather ridiculous compliment. But his evident sincerity and lack of any pretentiousness made it seem merely an expression of his natural modesty. After the ceremony, we had arranged for the choristers to sing for him. They stood in two rows in the nave, and after they had sung he went down the front row shaking hands with every boy. He then said, "Won't you sing me another verse?" When they did so he did exactly the same again, shaking hands with every boy in the second row. All this seemed of a piece with a character of exceptional humanity and courtesy. Yet it was the same man who, next day, addressed both Houses of Parliament in a speech displaying a statesmanship that could scarcely be equaled by any of our own political leaders. We were conscious of having met, on extraordinarily personal terms, one of the great world leaders of our century. His visit was a hard act to follow for the royal family or other heads of state who came afterwards, whose visits, by comparison, seemed strangely colorless and impersonal.

Of another kind altogether was the experience of entertaining Dom Helder Camara, the charismatic archbishop of Olinda and Recife in North East Brazil. It had arisen quite unexpectedly. Julian had long been entranced by his writings, particularly his short poetic meditations — he always denied being a poet, but he shared a poetic gift with other Latin American church leaders, and his "night thoughts" were undeniably prose poems. Julian was about to give a talk on him to an Abbey society, and asked me to find out more for her. I rang Westminster Cathedral, and was given the bare facts of his life and ministry. Half an hour later the phone rang again. "Dom Helder is coming to London in a few weeks' time to speak at a conference. Would you be able to have him for the night?" It seemed astonishing that this request should be coming from the R.C. church authorities to an Anglican clergyman. It made me realize how pervasive the Vatican's disapproval of Liberation Theology and all progressive movements of the church in Latin America had been. Of course we assented, and I rapidly arranged a small meeting in the Jerusalem Chamber for him to talk about his work for social justice worldwide, and also a dinner party for a few chosen people to meet him informally. All of this passed leaving a vivid impression of his modest yet inspiring personality; but the real excitement came next morning. Julian said afterwards that he must have spent the night either on the floor or in horizontal levitation above the bed: there was no sign of it having been slept in; and his cassock had so many buttons down the front she could not imagine how he could have taken it off and put it on again unaided. When he came down to breakfast, looking fresh and alert, his conversation with me and my family was unforgettable — intimate, sensitive, and, when he talked about his work among the poor, deeply moving. We have a photograph of him outside the house admiring a tall blue delphinium. As he did so he praised God for its beauty in a way reminiscent of St. Francis. Indeed we felt almost as if it had been St. Francis himself who had stayed the night with us.

These were just a few of the special moments that surface from memories of our routine, which included inviting and entertaining visiting preachers, attending or conducting Abbey services, participation in official Abbey occasions, and a regular round of administrative work. The Abbey was in some ways a place of great freedom, allowing one to work according to one's own preferred rhythm, in others a relentless master, one event or duty succeeding another with few breaks for sustained reflection or exploration. Yet it offered unrivalled opportunities for access to the higher echelons of government and Whitehall (letters headed "Westminster Abbey" seldom failed to receive attention), for creating common ground between people or movements that had fallen out with one another (the Jerusalem Chamber, where I hosted many meetings, had an extraordinarily irenic atmosphere), and for bringing a wider perspective of faith and reflection to those working in many different areas of public life.

When I arrived at the Abbey as the junior canon, I was appointed canon steward, which meant, among other things, supervising the hospitality that we offered. We were instructed on arrival that the tradition of a Benedictine monastery that we had inherited implied a ready welcome to all comers and a generous level of hospitality. For this we were given a small allowance for entertaining in our own houses — a slightly spurious application of the Benedictine rule, since the medieval monastery would have left all entertaining to the abbot (who had his own facilities, including a dining hall, for the purpose) while the monks got on with their various occupations without concerning themselves with visitors. Nevertheless we gladly did what we could for the many guests and friends who came our way (at one stage Julian said she would soon be making soup in her sleep); but meanwhile the Abbey assumed the responsibility for more formal and corporate entertaining, and it was this that I was called upon to supervise. I rapidly became aware that the bulk of it seemed to take the form of meals and receptions offered to well-heeled people who could easily afford their own luxuries, while the indigent were left without invitation to anything. By way of correcting this bias, I became involved with the work that was being done for the homeless by literally hundreds of London charities, and instituted regular evenings in which those working in the charitable agencies could spend some time in the Abbey when it was empty in the evening (a magical experience that we were privileged to be able to enjoy and share with others), and could meet one another over a simple buffet meal in the Jerusalem Chamber. These occasions began to change the image of the Abbey: instead of seeming to be the province only of the better-off and the successful, it slowly came to be seen also as an institution that was known to welcome society's casualties and those who worked for them. Given the security precautions that needed constantly to be maintained for the sake of the Abbey's public ministry, there was no possibility of us offering shelter or sustenance to the homeless and the destitute themselves; but by providing a welcome, a meeting ground, and simple hospitality to those who were working for them we were able to give support and encouragement where it was much needed, as well as having the opportunity to perform some well-informed advocacy on their behalf with government ministers and senior civil servants.

Before the end of my time I was able to extend this service to another charitable sector. In 1996 legislation came into force which made a large number of asylum seekers literally destitute, and churches, mosques, and synagogues were faced with the challenge of helping them to survive. Again, there was little the Abbey could do directly, but we could bring together those trying to cope with this new emergency in much the same way as we had done for those working for the homeless. From this point on I found myself deeply involved with asylum seekers, both as individuals and collectively. It was an issue on which there was much to say to politicians and administrators, and once again my position at the Abbey gave me precious leverage for doing so. Indeed this was a concern that remained with me for some years after I had retired. My exposure to what appeared to me to be a flagrant injustice inflicted upon some of the most wretched people in the world, who had escaped terrible moments of persecution in their own countries and had a right to expect some humanity when they sought sanctuary here, led me to the conviction that government policy and its execution by officials of what is now called the U.K. Border Agency were having consequences that were unacceptable to the Christian conscience. Moved by this conviction, I played an active part in a multi-faith coordinating committee that was addressing many of the practical issues in London, and subsequently I helped to revive a virtually moribund ecumenical church body which was tasked to do the same on a national scale. Here again there was an opportunity to bring my theological and philosophical training to bear on what I had come to believe was a moral as much as a political and administrative problem, and I used my position until I retired to promote the interests of the sufferers as much as I could. In this way I was finding a stage on which to play the part that I had always hankered for, that of a theologian whose faith was being brought to bear on the urgent problems of the world around. And I subsequently gave expression to the theoretical as well as the practical aspects of these inhumane policies (and the animosities frequently being aroused by the popular press) in a book, *Asylum in Britain: A Question of Conscience*, which was published in 2008.

Both Michael Mayne as dean, and myself as sub-dean, brought to completion projects that were particularly close to our hearts in the last years of our respective times at the Abbey. In 1996 there was unveiled a memorial to the Innocent Victims of Oppression, Violence and War. This was something that Dean Mayne had been working on for several years. It was becoming increasingly obvious that in modern armed conflict the principal sufferers were likely to be civilians; and while the grave of the Unknown Warrior, just inside the Abbey's main entrance, was acknowledged as the focus of national remembrance for the military casualties of war, something was needed to complement it as a reminder of the immense cost of conflict being paid by innocent women, children, and men. The first proposal was for a statue of a clearly frightened woman, looking back over her shoulder at some threatening calamity behind her, leading a child who was confidently straining to move forward into the future. A model was made by a gifted Irish sculptor (Ken Thompson), but after much discussion was rejected by bodies such as the Fine Arts Commission, mainly on the grounds that there were enough statues in the area already. Instead, we were allowed to place a large circular tablet below the western towers, bearing the inscription, "REMEMBER All Innocent Victims of Oppression Violence War" with a text on the border running around it that reads, "Is it nothing to you, all you that pass by" — a choice of text that had given us some trouble. The dean had proposed "God is our hope and strength." But I had protested: it was precisely the agonizing perception that God seemed *not* to be their hope and strength that had been part of the tragedy of the victims of the Holocaust. So we settled on the text from the Book of Lamentations.

The ceremony of unveiling by the queen was memorable, not least because we had gathered a group consisting both of survivors of extreme violence and oppression and of persons who had given notable service to them (such as Helen Bamber, the indomitable founder of the Foundation for the Care of Victims of Torture, now known simply as Freedom from Torture). This small group, standing outside the Abbey and close to the memorial alongside the queen and the Duke of Edinburgh, made for a scene of extraordinary poignancy, in startling contrast to the stiff uniformed figures who would normally be prominent at a formal ceremony commemorating a wartime event.

There had also been another change outside the west front of the Abbey. Some years before, our architect had made us think about the fact that there would be an expanse of plain stone at the foot of the north western tower once the restoration, then in progress, was completed. Should we not write something on it, a kind of "mission statement" for the Abbey? What a subject for long discussions in chapter meetings! In the end it was I who chanced on an answer. Churchgoers will be familiar with a form of words that has long been adopted as a blessing said at the end of a service. But I had also heard it in Oxford in its original Latin form, that of a grace after meals dating back to the time of Queen Elizabeth I. This had a punch line at the end which had been made anodyne in the modern adaptation: instead of "to us his servants" it originally read "to us *sinners*." The lines (with slight adaptation) then ran as follows:

> God grant
> to the living, grace,
> to the departed, rest,
> to the church and the world, peace and concord,
> and to us sinners, everlasting life.

This seemed to sum up quite well what the Abbey is all about: grace for all who come to it, rest for those who have died (an immense number of whom are buried or memorialized in the Abbey), peace and concord (which is the subject of our prayers every day), and finally, giving a salutary jolt at the end, a prayer for *us sinners* — which is indeed exactly what we all are. Inscribed in superb lettering at the bottom of the tower next to the main entrance, it is an arresting statement of the purpose of what goes on inside.

But my own project was more ambitious. When the twenty-five year work of restoration of the outside of the Abbey was nearly complete, our architect pointed out that there were ten empty medieval niches above the west door that were clearly intended for statues but which appeared never to have been filled. He insisted that the restoration would not be complete unless we put this right. But whom should the statues be of? There were few of the great figures of the past connected with Westminster Abbey who did not already have a statue somewhere. Should they not therefore have a more contemporary relevance? I had recently become aware that the twentieth century had seen more Christians killed because of their faith than any other period of history — there were more martyrs under Stalin alone than in the persecutions of the first Christian centuries. This was not widely known. Might we not use the empty niches to proclaim a message: that the century that was coming to its end had been the Century of Martyrdom? My colleagues accepted the proposal, and we set to work to make a choice from the many names which occurred to us. Clearly it was not a question of "the top ten." We needed to find those who best represented the persecution that had taken place in each part of the world, of whatever nationality or Christian denomination. We consulted with local church authorities in each continent, we did our own research and we sought the views of church historians. In the end we came up with ten names that would be seen as representative and would not arouse controversy (though there were inevitably questions about Martin Luther King and his private life, but in the event there was no criticism).

Five of these martyrs had suffered death explicitly for their Christian faith. Elizabeth of Russia, though a grand-daughter of Queen

Victoria and daughter-in-law of the tsar of Russia, was murdered by the Bolsheviks because she had become founder and member of a community of nuns, not because she was a royal person; Manche Masemola, a sixteen-year-old girl, was killed as disloyal to her animist family in South Africa in 1928; Lucian Tapiedi, a Papuan who worked with Anglican missionaries in Papua New Guinea, was killed by the Japanese invaders in 1942; Esther John, having been converted to Christianity and working as a Christian evangelist in Pakistan, was murdered in 1960, almost certainly as an apostate by members of her Muslim family; and Wang Zhiming, a Protestant pastor, was executed in the Cultural Revolution in China.

But of the others it could certainly be said that they did not all meet their death in the strict sense of Christian martyrdom: they were not all killed *because* they were Christians. Oscar Romero in El Salvador (assassinated by the government because of his championship of the poor), Janani Luwum in Uganda (killed by Idi Amin for promoting the church's resistance to the tyrannical demands of the régime), Dietrich Bonhoeffer in Nazi Gemany (executed because of his alleged involvement in the plot against Hitler's life), Maximilian Kolbe (interned and gassed in Auschwitz), Martin Luther King (assassinated for his part in combating racism in the USA) — these were all men who risked their lives for principles of justice and compassion rather than for explicitly defending the faith, which was the traditional definition of a martyr. But the motivation of all these was certainly Christian: they were inspired and sustained to the end by their faith. In the end Cardinal Basil Hume, the archbishop of Westminster, who at first declined our invitation to the ceremony on the grounds that "martyr" in official Roman Catholic doctrine implied "saint," and few of our ten "martyrs" qualified as recognized saints, was brought around (after quite a long correspondence with me) to this more recent understanding of Christian martyrdom, which was indeed already gaining ground in the Roman Catholic church.

The next and more difficult step was to have the statues made, and to have them in place in time for an unveiling that had to be arranged well in advance. One possibility was to have a public competition; but this option was rejected on the sensible grounds that more than one sculptor would be needed and it would be inappropriate to have a variety of styles (we had visions of lumps of concrete and constructions of twisted wire being thought to be the style demanded by modern artistic taste). Instead, our architect insisted on using the team of sculptors that had been working for some time on renewing the carvings on the outside of the Abbey and were already very skilled in architectural sculpture. The result was a set of outstanding statues which, in the event, aroused no aesthetic criticism — though that of the Indian girl Esther John seemed to us to be inferior to the others and we even thought for a while of replacing her. But in fact the ten have aroused consistent interest and admiration ever since they were placed in their prominent position over the Great West Door.

It soon became clear that this was not a project that should be done piecemeal or completed without ceremony. The archbishop of Canterbury should be asked to perform the unveiling, and the queen should be present, along with diplomats and church leaders from all the countries represented. We were also anxious that individuals who were in any way connected with the martyrs — relatives, friends or guardians of their memory — should have a chance to attend, and a fund was raised to pay travel expenses and hospitality for those from poorer countries. All our guests from abroad were offered accommodation in Westminster School, and there was a two-day festival of lectures and a concert, culminating in the service itself followed by a lunch for all in a marquee in the garden.

The service of dedication was inspirational. A long procession filed in through the Great West Door of clergy, religious and lay people from many parts of the world, and as I stood watching them I sensed that this was a celebration of a very different kind from our usual commemorations, with many people present whose lives had been touched by the martyrs we were celebrating. The congregation was seated around a central space in the nave, where the readings, the prayers, and the music took place. One of the lessons was read by the wife of Bishop Dehqani-Tafti, whose son had been martyred in Iran; another by a friend of Oscar Romero (whose brother was also present), a third by an Australian woman closely associated with those martyred with Lucian Tapiedi in New Guinea in 1942; and a movement from a Bach solo cello suite was played by Dietrich Bethge, the godson of Dietrich Bonhoeffer. At a certain point a small group of us went outside to witness the unveiling with the queen and the archbishop, along with those who had personally known or been connected with the martyrs (the Duke of Edinburgh was actually the great-nephew of one of them, Saint Elizabeth of Russia). As we stood there waiting for the great tarpaulin that covered the statues to be lowered, I had a nightmarish apprehension: would one of them immediately say, "But he didn't look like that at all!"? But our sculptors had done their work thoroughly from a careful study of the available photographs. All agreed that the statues were excellent likenesses, even including Lucian Tapiedi, for whom no photograph could be found and who had to be represented by a typical Papuan figure. By an extraordinary chance a small photo turned up just before the ceremony, and the statue was found to be remarkably like him!

The ceremony also had wider repercussions. Oscar Romero was shot by an assassin in 1980 while he was standing behind the altar in a chapel celebrating mass (the first bishop to have been killed officiating in a church since Thomas à Becket). Roberto d'Aubuisson, the leader of the ruling ARENA party, had been found to be implicated in the assassination by an international commission of inquiry. But his government persisted in denigrating the archbishop's memory so far as it could, refusing to give any compensation to his family and resisting all demands for an apology. When the Salvadorian ambassador in London received an invitation to a ceremony that would be attended by the queen of England honoring a Salvadorian citizen, he could hardly refuse to be there. And the news that Romero had received this honor on a prestigious international occasion soon travelled back to his country. There the government had grudgingly to come to terms with the fact that Romero had become a respected world figure. Nor did it end there. Some years later, after I had retired, I received an anxious message from Gaspar, Oscar Romero's brother, telling me about a proposal to honor D'Aubuisson with a statue in a public square in San Salvador. He himself was dead, but his party was still dominant in the country and the proposal had strong support in parliament. I responded by writing a letter for the dean of Westminster to send to the Salvadorian ambassador, expressing surprise that such a person's memory should be honored when he had been found responsible for the death of a churchman who was so widely revered that his statue had been placed on the front of Westminster Abbey in the presence of the queen and high ranking persons from all over the world. The letter was sent, and for a while nothing was heard in reply. Then, one day, the current ambassador (now a woman) announced that she would like to visit the Abbey. A private tour was arranged for her, at the end of which she suddenly produced a photographer and television crew, who captured her image gazing with evident approval at the statue. This too was publicized in her country, and the proposal to erect a statue to D'Aubuisson was quietly dropped. And even that was not quite the end of the story. Romero is now universally regarded as a saint in Latin America — he is referred to as "San Romero," even though the Vatican has not yet proceeded to canonize him.[1] When Pope Benedict was entering the Abbey during his visit in 2010, the dean drew his attention to Romero's statue by pointing it out to him above their heads. That moment was caught by the cameras, and was gratefully received by the faithful in El Salvador as a strong hint to the pope that he should get on with creating an official saint of "San Romero."

This dedication was the last major occasion I took part in before leaving the Abbey. The dean, Wesley Carr, had been appointed as Michael Mayne's successor when the preparations were already well advanced, and he generously left it to me to master-mind the events and preach at the service. The success of it was something of which I could justifiably be proud, though the project could never have been completed without the enthusiastic collaboration of our architect (Donald Buttress) and many others of the Abbey staff. I had also been greatly helped by Sister Hilary Markey, a Wantage Sister who worked as a pastoral assistant at the Abbey and had become one of our closest friends. She was expert in exploiting the many interna-

1. His beatification, the last stage in the process before canonisation, took place in 2015.

tional connections afforded by the missionary work of her order, and by the numerous visitors from abroad whom she got to know both at the Abbey and at St. Paul's Cathedral, where she also worked as a part-time assistant. It was she who was able to identify the martyr who would best represent southern Africa, the sixteen-year-old girl Manche Masemola, who was beaten to death in 1928 by her animist parents for working with an Anglican missionary, and is venerated at a shrine in the Transvaal. This choice was warmly endorsed by the South African church, and indeed the story had a poignant sequel that brought Manche into closer connection with the Abbey. Nearly half a century after killing her daughter, Manche's mother repented and was converted to Christianity. She was baptized by none other than Edward Knapp-Fisher, who was bishop of Pretoria and then canon and sub-dean of Westminster. He was my immediate predecessor, who had been a neighbor and friend in our first years at the Abbey.

My other source of support and encouragement was a gifted young historian, Andrew Chandler, from Birmingham University, who did serious research on all the proposed martyrs and edited the collection of essays by other experts which was published at the same time as the ceremony (*The Terrible Alternative*, 1998). I had met this historian at a conference he had organized in Birmingham on the Christian resistance to Hitler in Germany in the years up to the Second World War. This was a field in which he had specialized, and indeed he knew personally a number of the survivors. The conference had a distinctive character, the relatively small number of formal sessions being interspersed with cultural events, particularly the music of Bach, which was such a rooted feature of the culture of those whom we were commemorating. When I located him at the conference — he is one of the most modest and retiring people I have known, and was always in the back row or lurking in a corridor — I realized his unusual talent and brought him into our project. By this time he was working on founding a scholarly association that before long became the George Bell Institute, named after the principled and often controversial war-time bishop of Chichester. It was dedicated to the support, personal interaction, and friendship of scholars who were unsupported by universities in many parts of the world, were highly qualified in their own fields, and persevered in research that, for them, was a matter of conviction and faith. This was the kind of association I had dreamed of since I was young and had never found. I was glad to be involved with it from the beginning and have remained an admiring member of it ever since.

When I look back at my seventeen years at the Abbey I have to ask myself whether I made good use of the time. I certainly fulfilled the normal expectations of engagement with affairs outside the Abbey itself. One of these was my work in the commission which in 1985 produced the report, *Faith in the City* — a title that I dreamed up one night and which was enthusiastically adopted by my colleagues on the commission. The title was deliberately ambiguous — we had found faith alive and active in the cities we visited, and had also found our own faith in them strengthened by the resilience of many of the churches and Christian organizations we visited. The archbishop's commission that produced the report was given two years to do its work, and very hard work it was. We spent weekends in a number of cities where inner city deprivation, replicated also in some of the outlying areas, was particularly horrifying; we spent other weekends together sharing our views and experiences and formulating our conclusions. We did much of our work in smaller groups, visiting schools, prisons, and social agencies and concentrating on specific aspects of the crisis in inner cities and outlying estates that had been brought to the government's attention by riots in Toxteth, Brixton, and elsewhere. It is fair to say that none of us was the same person after the experience. We had witnessed a degree of alienation from the life of society, of isolation, and destitution, of which we, like most of the population, had been totally unaware.

We also witnessed remarkable vitality and determination among churches in some of the most destitute areas. On many of our visits we received an intensely warm welcome: people clearly expected that we could do something to help. This gave us a clue to the kind of report we should present. We were a church commission, though it was the expert competence of our members in many aspects of social and economic life, and the amount of hard work we all invested in it, which prevented our report from being disregarded when it was published (in the event it sold 24,000 copies, a record for a church report). But it was also written with a degree of passionate conviction. We had been horrified to discover what we came to call a "grave and fundamental injustice" in the conditions under which so many deprived city-dwellers lived. How should we respond to it? There were those of us who thought that, as a body of Christians, we should contrast what we had seen with a Christian vision of the ideal city, and challenge the government to move in that direction. But others, and in particular our excellent and extremely experienced chairman (Sir Richard O'Brien), were convinced that this would allow the politicians to dismiss our project as merely visionary and impractical, which would be a betrayal of all the victims of the situation who had looked to us to be an agent of practical change. This second view prevailed. Accordingly our report contained practical recommendations that we believed could be realized in the existing political climate.

Nevertheless, as a church-inspired document, it needed to be undergirded by principles drawn from the Christian faith; and this was the task given to me. After much thought and discussion, I concluded that it would be quite inappropriate to devise a theological rationale and impose it upon the realities we had witnessed. There was no need to justify our plea for action. It was a matter primarily of an injustice that could be seen by all and that demanded reform. The parable of the Good Samaritan was sufficient to provide a challenge to both "the church and the nation" (the sub-title of our report made it clear that we were addressing both). As for a deeper theological foundation, I believed that this must be explored and formulated, not in academic institutions, but by those who were wrestling with the problems in their own localities: "local theology" became one of our slogans. As a result, the "theological chapter," which was mainly my work, though it had been intensively discussed and firmly endorsed by my fellow commissioners, was widely criticized afterwards for having been "weak on theology." But in the event it resulted in an impetus being given, as we hoped it would, to many local initiatives of a theological kind. It also received an unexpectedly wide readership when two pages of the theater program for David

Hare's play "Racing Demon" at the National Theatre were devoted to an extended quotation from it! At the other extreme, the chapter was labelled "Marxist" in the campaign launched by the government to rubbish our report — a campaign that ultimately did us good, for it gave us a great deal more publicity than would normally follow the publication of a church document. As for Marxism, it is true that I had been much influenced by Liberation Theology, which had itself been partly inspired by a Marxist analysis of the very different social and economic situation in Latin America; but the notion that I was a Marxist seemed simply laughable to all who knew anything of my character and my work.

This must have been the first time that I was personally exposed to intensive attention from the media. The second followed a few years later. It all began in a quite unexpected way. I had written two articles for a journal called *Theology*, which appeared every two months and had a readership of a few thousand clergy and lay people — not the sort of publication that would normally attract the attention of the world at large. In these articles I had drawn attention to the fact that the church's teaching on marriage, divorce and sex outside marriage had fallen seriously behind society's practice; as a result, the clergy are "caught in a dilemma. They cannot deny the church's traditional teaching on these matters; yet if they continue to teach it they know it will not be observed; and they risk either giving a bad conscience to young people for doing what in their hearts they believe to be right, or else, by their implicit condemnation, discouraging the great majority of 'normal' people from having anything more to do with the Church." I went on to show that the teaching of Jesus and St. Paul is by no means unambiguous, and certainly does not support a doctrine of indissolubility (which in any case had already been abandoned by the Church of England); nor does it make explicit mention of sex outside marriage (apart from with prostitutes), indeed sexual relations between a betrothed couple were not condemned in Jewish society and are nowhere explicitly forbidden in the Bible. Consequently, I argued, the church should "cease pressing individual, and for the most part problematic, texts into the service of maintaining a legalistic and increasingly disregarded code of behaviour."

Journals of this kind have quite a long lead time between accepting an article and publishing it, and in any case I was not expecting this one to cause any sort of stir. I was not the first to express such views, and the church was already beginning to move towards a more liberal position. It was a surprise, therefore, in the autumn of 1993, to be rung up towards midnight by *The Times* and told that I and my allegedly radical views were featured prominently on the front page of next morning's papers. What had happened was that the *Church Times* had thought my first article interesting enough to publish some long excerpts from it; and these were picked up by the national press on the assumption that, if things like this were being said by a senior cleric on the staff of Westminster Abbey, he must be challenging official doctrine and breaking ranks with his superiors — in short, a good story. Within hours it was all around the world; and all next day the telephone rang continuously with calls from as far afield as Vancouver and Sydney. Amidst the pandemonium of that day, two interviews stick in my mind. One was with an admirable reporter from the *Evening Standard*, who brought Julian into it and had us photographed together in front of the Abbey, I in my full clerical dress and Julian with her hair flowing freely in the wind, under the headline, "He's very rash, says Canon's wife" — he had extracted this by taking Julian aside when I was not looking! The other was on Radio 4, when I was invited to have a discussion with a bishop who would take a different view from mine. When I arrived at the studio the presenter looked embarrassed and told me that the bishop had not been available after all, and they had asked "someone else." When I went in, the "someone else" turned out to be the redoubtable Christian debater and politician Ann Widdecombe. She was already seated on one side of the table, and was staring fixedly at a copy of the King James Bible open in front of her. She lost no time in laying into me on the grounds that I had got the biblical texts wrong. Unfortunately for her, she had chosen the wrong text: St. Matthew's gospel, the one she was reading from, gave more support to my position than to hers. I have unfortunately never met her since to continue the conversation. By the next day, of course, it was all over, and life became normal again. When I published a short book expanding my position (*Promise or*

Pretence?, 1994) it attracted little notice. But the experience, though interesting and not unduly unpleasant for me, gave me a daunting impression of what it must be like for any private individual to be seriously involved in a personal tragedy or scandal that has caught the world's attention.

Wesley Carr, the third dean under whom I served, was appointed in 1997, and within a few months had the delicate and highly public task of supervising the arrangements for Princess Diana's funeral, for which he received well-deserved commendation. Negotiations between the royal family and the Spencers had not been easy, but the result was acclaimed as extremely impressive and indeed moving. It was one of the occasions when one became aware of the strength of the Abbey's traditions, the instinctive teamwork of the staff, and the long experience that helped to fashion each new event. Count-less funerals have taken place there, from the most modest to the most splendid, and each has built upon the experience of the pre-vious ones. From our point of view, the procedures were in place, just as for any other funeral; what was exceptional this time was the extraordinary surge of public emotion and the sense that every detail of the service would be scrutinized in the light of the controversy surrounding both the life and the death of the princess. Julian and I were on holiday in France when the tragic death occurred, and flew back immediately. By then the details had been settled, and my own role was minimal apart from the ceremony itself, in which it was my privilege to accompany the queen into her place in the Abbey and out again for the departure of the coffin. At this later moment I was standing beside her at the West Door watching the departure of the hearse, and a photograph of the scene quickly went around the world and appeared in the glossy weeklies of many countries. It had just been published when we returned to continue our holiday in France, and it was quite hard for the local newsagent to believe that the cleric so prominently escorting the queen of England on the front page of his magazine was the same person as the informally dressed tourist in front of him. I had been able to spend some of the night before the funeral talking to the people who, in their hundreds, were camping on the pavement near the Abbey, and had derived from them a sense of the emotions they felt. When the service took place, the doors of the Abbey were left wide open and there were loudspeakers broadcasting it to the crowds outside. At the end of Earl Spencer's address they started applauding, and the applause slowly spread through the doors and up the length of the Abbey to where we and the royal party were seated. Since the address had been openly critical of the treatment Diana had received from the Palace, the moment was acutely embarrassing. Seated as we were a few feet from the queen, we could hardly join in the applause; yet by then the entire congregation had done so, and we were left in awkward isolation with her and her family. But this was the only moment when we had any anxiety. The ceremony went off smoothly — despite the guardsmen swaying uncertainly under the weight of a lead coffin — and there were moments of great beauty. It had been a heavy week for the new dean; but I was able to remark to him afterwards that the outcome, which was generally applauded, must have left no doubt in his mind, or anyone else's, that he was now indeed the Dean of Westminster.

But this event was soon followed by another of a very different kind that gave the Abbey less welcome publicity. We had recently appointed a new auditor, whose first audit contained questions about the accounts of the music department, for which our distinguished organist, Martin Neary, was responsible. The questions related to the choir's engagements outside the Abbey and its tours abroad: had the fees been properly negotiated and accounted for? When something of this kind took place, the normal procedure was for the member of staff concerned to be immediately suspended until investigations could take place; and in this case all the professional advice we received was that we must follow it, even though Martin Neary was a senior member of the "Collegiate Body." We had hoped, perhaps naively, that Martin might go away to his country cottage for a long weekend, allowing us to establish the facts in his absence and settle the matter privately. But we had not reckoned with his temperament, or indeed with the fact that, being a prominent professional musician, he could not regard the threatened suspension as anything but an outrageous injustice, and instantly alerted all his friends in high places. The result was that what we had hoped might be a private matter that could be resolved quietly became overnight a widely publicized dispute, all the more regrettable in that it was between a church and its employee. We had long and fruitless negotiations, and then Martin appealed to the queen, as he was entitled to do as a member of a royal foundation. The queen appointed a retired judge to hold a judicial inquiry, which went on for several weeks and was a painful experience for those of us who were required to give evidence. It also cost both parties a great deal of money, and had dire consequences for the Abbey's reputation. In the end the judge found that Martin was at fault and could not claim to be reinstated, though he also expressed some criticism of the way the Abbey had handled the matter.

All this time Martin had been living in his official residence next door to ours. We had the embarrassment of passing him in frosty silence in the cloisters, while dark-suited professionals were visiting him at home, helping him to prepare his case against us. He had been a good neighbor and a good friend, indeed he had helped me greatly in the preparations for the concert that was part of the martyrs' festival. For many nights I lay awake agonizing over whether all this could have been avoided; some were saying that the dean had been unduly rigid, and even that he had allowed personal dislike to influence his stance. But it had become obvious quite early on that no compromise was possible. I felt bound to the conclusion that we had taken the only possible course of action: Martin had undoubtedly precipitated a situation which we could not allow to continue. When it was all over I found it extremely painful to have parted in this way from someone who had been a friend and whom I had admired and respected for his artistic gifts; and I always hoped for some opportunity to tell him so. But although I have been able to have friendly conversations with his wife and daughter, no opportunity has occurred for me to make my peace with him.

In 1999, a year after the dedication of the martyrs' statues, I was nearly seventy (the official retiring age) and had been at the Abbey for a full seventeen years. It was time to retire. A few months before leaving, I was asked to give some thought to my preferences with regard to leave-taking. Early in my time, when I was canon steward, I had acquired a reputation for a certain austerity. I had put an end,

for instance, to serving cigars and cigarettes at the end of formal dinners offered by the Abbey (this was still the custom in those days of
reckless smoking) and had reduced the amount of wine served to
guests after one or two members of staff had clearly over-indulged
themselves. Certainly I was always anxious to make sure that our
hospitality, though it might be generous, should never be ostenta-
tious or extravagant. Two of my colleagues had recently left before
me, and I was shocked to discover what their departures had cost the
Abbey in dinner parties and large farewell receptions. So I attempted
to set a more modest style of leave-taking. I refused any special dinner parties, and asked that the customary lunchtime reception in a
marquee in the garden should offer simple sandwiches for lunch
accompanied by an innocuous cider cup and soft drinks instead of
the usual choice of wines. I had also asked that the occasion should
be relatively informal (without our usual Abbey uniform of red cassocks), and I caused genuine surprise by arranging for our guests to
be greeted at the door by a small steel band (I was good friends with
an enthusiastic black musician) and that after the necessary formal
speeches and presentations we should have some dancing, which got
going in earnest when, with my son-in-law at the piano, I struck up
the Blue Danube Waltz on my violin. I doubt whether there had ever
been such a leaving party before; I have not heard that there has been
since. But this one was certainly more enjoyable than most, not least
for our one-year-old grand-daughter, who joined delightedly in the
dancing, but also for a group of my friends among asylum seekers,
who I had insisted should be invited. For them, the occasion was undoubtedly a welcome diversion from the trials of their precarious
existence, which were to continue to occupy me for several years
after I had retired.

CHAPTER 8

Extension: Retirement in Willersey

O ne of the promises I had always made to Julian was that when
I retired she would not have to live in Willersey. It is a beautiful village in the Cotswolds, and, despite my promise, has turned
out to be the ideal place for us to retire to in a number of ways. But
Julian could not help having mixed feelings about it. Her maternal
grandmother came from a family that had lived in or near Willersey
for at least two hundred years, and her mother was brought up in
it. Her grandfather was also from the area: he was a gifted painter,
associated with the Broadway painters in the time of John Singer
Sargent; but his wife (Julian's grandmother) had no time for such
things and insisted he followed the career for which he was also qualified, that of an architect. Eventually he became borough surveyor for
Evesham: among other things he was responsible for laying out the
attractive Abbey Park there, with its ponds and little bridge. But he
died in his fifties when Jane, his eldest daughter, was only nineteen,
and Julian's grandmother became a widow for the next half-century.
When Julian first took me to see her, shortly before we got married
(somewhat nervously, since she was not sure how I would react), she
was already nearly eighty and had adopted an old-lady style of dress
that never changed — grey knitted skirts and cardigans over white
blouses; and her way of life and her character seemed similarly set.
She lived in a small seventeenth-century cottage at the end of a row
of what had once been farm laborers' cottages, with its front window
looking down the village street and with a small garden at the back.

There was no heating other than a fire in a tiny grate in the living room — Granny was said sometimes to leave the light on at night so that the heat from the small bulb in the ceiling should give some warmth to her bedroom above. Her diet was equally austere: one loaf of the locally baked wholemeal brown bread each week, with butter and regular cups of tea, was all she ever had, leaving it to relatives and neighbors to provide her with an occasional cooked meal — which they did readily, since she was well liked in the village; but they soon learned not to expect any show of gratitude. She affected an obstinate refusal to be helped in any way, such that those who supplied her needs had to do so against invariable resistance. In the end they found themselves thanking *her* for finally accepting, instead of being thanked themselves.

Next door to her (in another cottage she owned) lived her son, Julian's uncle — or at least would have done, had he not been normally abroad, serving in the British Council. Henry had been at Oxford before the Second World War, where he made friends with a number of fellow students who subsequently became well-known writers. He combined great charm (especially felt by women), as well as a gift for sparkling and witty conversation, with a tendency to flare up into sudden bursts of anger and an ability to show what can only be called a will to inflict deliberate hurt (I do not think there was any adult member of his family — apart from his tough old mother — whom I did not see in tears after talking with him on at least one occasion). His relationship with the novelist Barbara Pym, which is recorded in her autobiography entitled A Very Private Eye — Henry is "Lorenzo" in that book — is typical of him: he allowed women to remain hopelessly attached to him without apparently being aware of any obligations in return. He was married twice, first to an aristocratic Swedish-Finnish lady, then to the daughter of a German Nazi-inclined pastor. Both marriages resulted in two children, both ended with a more or less painful divorce: the second was torn apart abruptly when, returning from London to Willersey on Christmas Eve, Henry found his two small sons abandoned on their own in the cottage, with no food or provisions, their mother having gone off with a lover in Scotland. The two daughters of the first marriage had returned to Finland with their mother; one of them became mentally ill and has spent the rest of her life in an institution. The two boys stayed with Henry and went to a public school and then Oxford, where they became infected with the spirit of the 'sixties and, to their father's despair, refused to compromise with the norms of society to the extent of settling down into a job.

In order to avoid a further posting abroad while his two sons were still at school, Henry had to retire at sixty and came to live in Willersey. Still at the height of his powers, but disinclined to take any job that might not be to his taste, he had little to do and his frustration turned into an obsession about the "point of join" between the two cottages and the boundary between them. Granny had by then gifted one of them to him and the other to Julian (on condition that she could continue living there herself until she died). We did our best to make her more comfortable by adding a room with a south window, so that she would at least have the sun to warm her, with a bathroom next to it; and she was able to continue living there until the end of her life. When she died in 1968 the cottage became ours, and we began to use it for holidays and occasional brief escapes from our routine at home. It was then that Henry's obsession over the two cottages began to cause real concern. Because we did not accede to his ideas for alterations in our kitchen (he wanted us to close up a window we regarded as indispensable) he accused us of obstruction and obfuscation, and in due course broke off relations altogether: we could communicate only through a solicitor. Julian did her best to circumvent this ridiculous restriction by tying a message for him around the neck of his cat; but to no avail! The atmosphere subsequently improved sufficiently for us to be able to meet and talk about anything not connected with the dispute, and indeed I looked forward to these conversations, which were humorous and stimulating; but the grudge against us remained until his death (he had left strict instructions that I should not be invited to conduct his funeral) and the dispute has gone on into the next generation. It has only recently been resolved.

Thus it is understandable that Julian should have been in two minds about retiring to live in Willersey. And there were other reasons against doing so. She was a painter and, despite having sold at least a hundred of her pictures and sketches in London, she still had a large stock of her work; and for my part I had amassed a library of about a thousand books which I was by no means ready to part with. All this, along with a grand piano and the furniture that had filled our large official houses, seemed to rule out a small Cotswold cottage as our retirement home. We had of course seen the problem long before, indeed we had been looking for the ideal house for many years. But a certain indecisiveness was part of Julian's character, and since there was no urgency we continued to prevaricate, even, on two occasions, withdrawing from a purchase at the very last minute. In the months before actual retirement we did of course begin to take the issue more seriously; but I allowed myself to be so busy up to the end of my time at the Abbey that we were still without a new house when the moment came to leave. There was no alternative to putting the greater part of our possessions in store and camping provisionally in the still spartan and restrictive conditions of our cottage.

With our Christmas card in 1999 we enclosed a note describing our situation as "The Harvey Equation," and briefly spelling out the arguments for and against settling down in Willersey. I lighted on a partial solution when I was able to acquire another small cottage in the next village. Having been built in the early nineteenth century as the lodge for a larger house, with solid stone walls and quite high rooms, it was ideal for housing books, pictures and the grand piano, as well as making a delightful annex for our family and guests to stay in. This did not altogether resolve our doubts, and we continued our long and fruitless search for the ideal house for some time; but the effect of gradually making friends and adapting to the village routine began to make us conscious of the advantages of settling in Willersey, and after a few years the "equation" ceased to trouble us. Recently, as Julian's mind began to fall prey to dementia, the help and support I have received from the village has more than justified our indecisiveness.

But in any case we still had some travelling in mind. Sehon Goodridge had by this time returned to the West Indies, having been forced to leave the valuable work he was doing for black clergy in London by being elected (without knowing he was being considered) bishop of St. Vincent. He was keen that I should go and do some lecturing for his clergy. His diocese encompassed several islands, and there would be a chance to see some of them. We began with St. Vincent itself, where Sehon lived in a house less imposing than that in Barbados, but gracious and comfortable, and where Janet had created a beautiful tropical garden. Up the road he had built a conference center for the diocese, and there he gathered substantial audiences for my lectures. Our visit coincided with anniversary celebrations of the island's independence, which included not just a big service in the cathedral, at which I was invited to preach, but a long open-air ceremony where I was given an embarrassingly prominent seat and was able to witness a powerful rendering of "Amazing Grace" by a lady who was a cabinet minister (something hard to imagine in England!) as well as a generous demonstration of the rhetorical skills of West Indian people. We then went on to Antigua, where the church warden of the parish that was sponsoring us happened to be the assistant manager of a luxury hotel on the coast. As a result we were accommodated in conditions we would never have dreamt of enjoying — a little chalet near the beach and a central area for meals, drinks, and almost anything else we could have wished for, all free of charge. This little paradise lasted a week; for our second week we were the guests of the manager of the town's bookshop, a cultivated man who played the flute and showed us wonderful hospitality.

The smaller island of St. Kitts was also on our itinerary. I was keen to go there because it was where my father's mother had been brought up. A certain John Pogson had raised a troop of horse for Charles I, who had paid for it by the grant of a stretch of land in St. Kitts — we saw his fine marble tombstone in the church nearby. He prospered, despite the unfavorable climate (the estate was in the lee of a mountain so that it did not receive the trade wind which brought health and refreshment elsewhere); and the estate passed from father to son right up to the end of the nineteenth century. My grandmother, one of seven sisters with no brothers, came to England when the estate was sold (there being no male heir), and married my grandfather who became a prominent financier in the city. The Pogson family must, of course, have been slave owners and subsequently employers of indentured laborers, who were often treated at least as badly as the slaves. My great-grandfather, however, seems to have been a humane man. One day he saw a black woman giving birth with great difficulty in the open country. In response he built and endowed a cottage hospital in the village for the local people. When we went to St. Kitts we were lodged with an English missionary and his wife whose house was just down the road from the hospital, and I was able to visit it. I also saw the deeds of gift, and noticed to my dismay that if the building ceased to be used for its original purpose it must be returned to whoever was the surviving male heir of the family. This, I believed, must be me, and since there were rumors that the government was going to close the hospital, I saw the dismal prospect of being involved in protracted litigation. Fortunately the government changed its mind and the hospital is now prospering.

It was quite by chance that we found ourselves staying in Sandy Bay, the very place where the Pogsons had settled, and the ruins of their house were only a few hundred yards away. I had heard reports of this house having a distinctive feature that was octagonal. Little remained of the house other than a few walls, but the octagonal part was clearly visible, and I could then understand the point of it. At the ground floor level it had slits for windows and was clearly a little fortress. And this was prudent. St. Kitts was the scene of frequent skirmishes between the French and English in the seventeenth and eighteenth centuries, and for a while had been divided between the two nations: the French had the extremities (where the place names are still French) the English the central part. Sandy Bay, the Pogsons' village, was near the northern frontier of the English section, and it was prudent to be well fortified, not just against forays from the French, but also against marauding Spanish ships.

St. Kitts' territory includes the small adjacent island of Nevis, a strategic point in Nelson's Caribbean campaigns, where he also found and married a wife. There is now a Horatio Nelson museum in Charlestown near Government House. One of the parishes is the domain of an archdeacon, and we were invited to spend a night there so that I could give a lecture to what turned out to be a very small gathering of extremely miscellaneous church people. But the visit is best described by Julian in her diary:

Now it was the ferry, small, clean, and not even for cars. I was helped on by two strong sailors, and then I watched, fascinated, those coming on. A tall black lady, in a long dark coat, fine hat, and dress carefully embroidered with small red flowers, her luggage, green and elegant, which the two strong sailors could scarcely lift — naturally commanding, she was surely a citizen of Nevis. On deck there was a Turneresque sky that seemed to create strange forms. One was like a Greek hero, swiftly painted, but not long to stay. We passed those wild desolate places at the end of St. Kitts; and now it was sunset, and only us and the sea.

On the small quay taxi men shouted into our ears, until suddenly we were greeted by an enormous man, wide and strong of body, Canon Percival — Anthony recognized him from his seminars in St. Kitts. "We'll take the long way round," he said, "it's not dark yet." A careful driver — sharp-cornered roads, the sea on one side, and undimmed headlights caused him no worry. "Now," he said, "if we go a rather bumpy way...." Darker now, we stopped in a flat field. Not far away, a small church of grey stone. It was ruined, but it still had a graciousness about it. No houses near, just this flat meadow in front with the dim rise of a tree-clad mountain behind. Canon Percival told us it had been commissioned by a planter called Cottle who had been determined that his black labourers should take part in the same service as himself and his family. He cared for them, and had been shocked by the cruelty of another planter called Edward Huggins, who had flogged his labourers in the town centre, killing two of them. That little church had still the Cottle spirit. Rather sadly, the Canon said, "There is thought of restoring it." Obviously it was precious to him.

Back now and down a steep way. "All my people live here," he said. In the twilight the tall crosses from the graveyard opposite were eerie. Avoiding two donkeys we swirled up a worn field. "Here we are. I've been here 17 years. I've worked on the house and improved it." Close by, a thin, wolf-like dog barked murderously (always chained, I knew). It took our host some time to open the door, and I turned to see all I could in the last light. A dark, threatening mountain, and in front of it one of those amazingly tall, narrow-stemmed palm trees, so wind-wracked that its cutting leaves were clearly visible against the last light, like one of George MacDonald's most sinister trees — it was "taking over," I thought.

Inside, a small boy, scrinny and unsmiling, watched a jazzily coloured something on TV. Lost and chilly, he seemed. No one spoke to him. We were to go up to see our room. "I did it myself," he said, "for people to stay in, so you should have all you need." The shuddering of that palm and the alien unresponsiveness of the boy came back to me as he showed us the room. Old nylon blue curtains were cut into old white ones. One could not open the window because of them (immediate claustrophobia!). Nor could one get to the other window, for a tall square plywood modern box — a what? It was a loo, so firmly put in place with the plywood (surely by himself) that to sit on it you could hardly shut the door. There was something of Wuthering Heights about it all, more modern, perhaps, but caught and held! I shivered. The boy, the dark palm about to assume its night powers, and this....

"How can you lecture tonight?" I asked Anthony. How he managed to talk to the people who sat round the long table in the barn room I don't know. They did not seem quite alive — except for one lovely old lady who sat next to me.

Next morning we would see the old town by the sea.... Later, the Canon took us over his fine, long church; fresh air coming through its open doors and tall lilies by the altar, it was beautifully kept. Soon Anthony found a marble monument. "Look!" he said, "this is Edward Huggins, the planter who was so cruel to his labourers — and look at this long list of his exceptional virtues!" Left to ourselves, we found the grave, carefully kept, of the same man. But few of these graveyards are fenced, so with hurricanes and always wandering animals it must be hard to keep them in order. Ironically (since I had just bought a picture of one in St. Kitts) I was put off by six donkeys, especially by one with a foal, tall and suspicious. Was this donkey akin to the sinister mountain, the brooding silence of the little boy, the palm tree beginning its different life at night, and (among the donkeys in the twilight) the strangely unhurt grave of Edward Huggins?

Very soon after we moved to Willersey I received an invitation which was to add a whole new dimension to my retirement. I have already recounted how the unveiling of a statue of Oscar Romero on the west front of Westminster Abbey had political implications for El Salvador. Romero was assassinated on March 24, 1980; and, as the twentieth anniversary approached, ambitious preparations were being made by the church to mark it with a worthy celebration. ARENA, the party whose leader instigated the murder of the arch- bishop, was still in power, and there was some apprehension that the government would seek to repress any large demonstration of public loyalty to their hero (at the time of his funeral around thirty people had been shot by the military in the square outside the cathedral). In the event these fears turned out to be groundless: there was no sign of military or police enforcement of public order. The plan was that there was to be an open air mass in a huge open space at one end of the city, followed by a procession for about two miles along a main highway to the large square outside the cathedral. This was to be the site of another great service, this time an ecumenical one with church leaders from all denominations and speeches from distinguished ecclesiastics who had been closely associated with Romero. To my surprise I was invited to be one of them, on the assumption that I could say something about the commemoration of Romero at West- minster Abbey.

Since, at the time I was invited, I knew no Spanish, this seemed a daunting prospect; but the idea of taking part in the celebration was exciting, and I agreed to go. I had only three months in which to learn enough Spanish to make my way in El Salvador and to give a speech to the thousands assembled in the cathedral square (by far the largest congregation I have ever addressed), followed by another lecture I was asked to give at short notice at a meeting in a hall. This was not altogether unrealistic. I had been for some time reasonably fluent in French, German, and Italian, but as I tried to learn Spanish on my own I began to feel baffled by problems of grammar and pronunciation. Some local classes in conversation (mainly for the benefit of travelers to Spain who would need to know how to book a room, order a beer or have their car repaired) were of little help. By chance I was then introduced to a Spaniard living only a few miles away who had taught Spanish in London for most of his life. He turned out to be not only a charming and cultivated man but also a brilliant teacher. In just a few lessons he gave me a sense of the language and a confidence that made acquiring a working knowledge in a few months seem practicable; and by dint of hard work I had reached a point by the time I left England at which I could converse in Spanish without too much embarrassment, and could also hold the attention — and apparently deserve the applause — of the immense gathering I found myself addressing outside the cathedral. This was gratifying in itself; but it also fulfilled one of the two ambitions I had cherished for my retirement. Learning Spanish was one of them, and finding I could now read the poetry of John of the Cross in the original language was an immediate reward. The other ambition was to be able to play string quartets. To my astonishment Willersey provided this also: a retired couple just down the road were both string players and a fourth was easily found. My first year of retirement seemed to indicate that living in Willersey was the right solution to our "equation."

During the week I spent in the city of San Salvador, I was the guest of Michael Campbell-Johnston, a Jesuit priest who had dedicated a lifetime of service to great causes — he was the founder of the international Jesuit Refugee Service in Rome, an agency that brought help to thousands of displaced people, and he became an influential player in the world of humanitarian work. He had recently taken over a parish in a poor quarter of the city where the priest and five young laymen had been assassinated by the regime and the church officially closed. He re-opened the church and made it a center of aid and education for the local children. He also won the trust of the young gangs in the neighborhood so as to have some protection for parish activities (El Salvador was the second most violent and lawless country in Latin America: after the recent civil war it was awash with small firearms, and the gangs of young men were, and still are, extremely powerful). He lived in just one very small room in the center of the compound, with children swirling around him, who loved him unreservedly and were rewarded by him being always available to them. Most of these children came from homes that were little more than corrugated iron shacks standing on a mud floor; but when they came out to school in the morning they all wore immaculate white shirts and were as merry as children brought up in luxury. My experiences among these vivacious and colorful people were as important to me as the official events of the week-long celebration; and when I encountered an English woman who had given all her resources of time and money to help establish a refuge for Salvadorian street children and whose life in England was entirely devoted to raising money for its support, I discovered that she lived only a few miles from Willersey. Doing what I can for her charity (ACES — Aid for Children of El Salvador) has become another of the strands in my quite active and varied retirement existence.

There was a third ambition at the back of my mind, though I had ceased to expect it to be fulfilled so late in life. I had never been to Africa, which seemed to me to be a serious omission. In my work for asylum seekers I had got to know many Africans. One such asylum seeker was a girl from the Congo (then Zaïre, now the DRC, the Democratic Republic of Congo), who had been forced to flee from Kinshasa without her husband and children and had no idea whether they were still alive. She became one of our most warmhearted friends and spent one Christmas with us in Willersey. I was able to speak for her at the tribunal which heard her case against deportation and at which we were successful. Through her I met Raphaël, also from Kinshasa, who was himself an asylum seeker (in due course he gained leave to remain) and was working in an agency for Francophone refugees at the French-speaking church close to Leicester Square. A devout catholic, who carried the cross for us in front of the cardinal archbishop during a Good Friday procession into Westminster Abbey, he appeared totally dedicated to the welfare of other Congolese in London. When in due course he acquired

British citizenship he felt safe enough to return to Kinshasa for a visit. He found the state of the country horrifying. After years of civil war the economy was in ruins, public services were paralyzed, there was no postal service, and virtually no judicial system. He had inherited a small compound in the city, and by the time he returned to London he had formed the idea of turning it into a home for street children, of whom there were some thirty thousand living without homes or families in Kinshasa alone. The next step was to found a charity to raise money, and I found he had already fixed upon me as chairman. He had also made friends with Lord Alton, who himself had founded a charity mainly concerned with vulnerable children in developing countries, and this charity took Raphaël's project under its wing, though leaving me to raise money for it. The first step was to visit Kinshasa and look at the practicability of the scheme. Accordingly the Jubilee Trust (David Alton's charity) made arrangements for David, myself, and a young assistant to go with Raphaël for a week to evaluate possibilities.

Despite the chaotic conditions in the city, Raphaël arranged and carried out our program with an efficiency and punctuality that we had hardly expected. Many of his former school friends, having compromised with the regime of the dictator Mobutu, had avoided the persecution that had killed Raphaël's father and best friend, and were now in senior positions in the government. Through these contacts Raphaël obtained interviews for us with leading authorities right up to one of the vice-presidents. As the one French speaker in the party, I had to be the spokesman on all formal occasions, and found myself making impromptu speeches explaining the purpose of our visit, which, being led by a British parliamentarian, had a diplomatic as well as a charitable side. These speeches were widely reported and may even have done some good for British-DRC relations. We were taken to see examples of the desperate state of some institutions: the general hospital, which used to be one of the finest on the continent, was partly ruinous, hopelessly under-provided with equipment and medicines, and staffed by dedicated doctors and nurses who seldom received any salary from the government.

We also saw some magnificent work being done by religious

orders for disabled children, and met representatives of the many international agencies trying to bring order into the chaos and help the country prepare for the first democratic elections held there since the first prime minister after Independence was overthrown in the coup that brought the dictator Mobutu to power. We were also introduced to a factor that had recently become prevalent and had increased the amount of homelessness among children. In cases where a family found it could no longer support all its children, if one of them showed signs of disability or deformity, or even if there had been a spell of bad luck for the family, the suspicion might arise that the child was a witch. He or she would then be expelled from the family and the community and end up on the streets. There were even ministers of fringe churches who claimed they could carry out an exorcism if they were paid an appropriate (usually extortionate) fee.

One of the most surprising of our visits was to the leader of the Katanguist Church, the third largest Christian denomination in Congo. I described it in the diary I was keeping of our visit.

Then came something quite extraordinary. Even Raphaël was taken by surprise. Part of our programme was to meet church leaders, and this morning it was to be the head of the third largest denomination, a Bible-based evangelical church started by the prophet Kitangu at the end of the nineteenth century. We drove into a large compound of smart green-and-white buildings, and as we got to the centre we saw a large brass band on one side and rows of neat green and white uniforms on the other, a crowd of several hundred standing round and a dais on the veranda with two rows of red plush chairs. I was firmly placed in the very front — fortunately I had put on jacket and collar in preparation for a later visit — and David and the others were in the second row behind me. The band burst into deafening sound, actually very well played, even if each piece was just a few bars played over and over again. Then came prayer and a reading and a hymn, followed by introductions, first of the officials and elders present (one was 104 years old), then of us, and after each introduction there was another blast from the band and an invocation of the Father (clap, clap, clap), the Son (clap, clap, clap) and the Holy Spirit (clap etc — we soon learnt how to join in). I was beginning to realize that a proper speech would be required and that it would have to be me. So I got up and did a French improvisation — thanks for the amazing reception, presentation of my colleagues, purpose of our visit, explanations, solidarity, mutual support, etc. It seemed to go well, with much appreciative nodding of ancient elders' heads, and my colleagues (who had not heard me hold forth like this before in French) were surprised and relieved. Then David did the same in English, which I translated as he went along, and gave them some excellent texts from the Bible to think about (should I have been doing that? But no, it came very well from him); and finally Raphaël spoke in Lingala, and whatever he said it went down well, with plenty of smiles and laughter. Another burst from the band, and we were ushered indoors to sit on deep upholstered chairs before the spiritual father of the church, a small portly man in a tight-fitting suit, perched on a sofa with a Buddha-like immobility. It turned out that he spoke only Lingala, so everything had to be translated into French or English by officials who knelt on the ground near him. The exchange was slow and inevitably banal, but we did get in a question about child witches, and received a straight answer: this church had always fought the devil in all his forms, including that of witchcraft. Finally David produced an appropriate gift from his pocket (a House of Lords clasp) and we said goodbye. But of course that was not the end. Outside we were put back in the plush chairs for photographs, there was another speech, and then the band started up in earnest, this time conducted by the tight-suited spiritual father himself. Soon it became still louder and the tempo quickened. People began waving white handkerchiefs (we were shown how to join in) and some were swaying and dancing slowly in long lines. All round were smiling, swaying people, with a scatter of brightly coloured umbrellas and women in bright African clothes — this was the moment I really knew I was in Africa!

When we had returned to England and given our report, the Jubilee Trust, our parent charity, decided that the project was viable; we began serious fund-raising and eventually raised around sixty thousand pounds. I had gathered a committee of experienced people: Lord Alton himself, a former head of two large comprehensive schools, a civil servant of African origin working on development issues, a senior diplomat from the DRC embassy, and the directors of the two national charities that successively supported us. We sent Raphaël to Kinshasa twice to oversee work on the renovation of the house and its adaptation for children, and four of us made a second visit to see for ourselves. This time we had a more modest program, which was intended to culminate in the first meeting of a strong local committee. This proved a disappointment: only one of its assumed members turned up. But we accepted that there were practical reasons for this (Kinshasa was in a period of considerable unrest: there were long power cuts despite the enormous potential of the Congo for hydro-electric generators, the young president had mysteriously not been seen for some weeks, and there were soldiers everywhere on the streets). In any case we returned to London reasonably confident about the way things were going. Our one real anxiety was about the country itself. Since our visit four years earlier there had been no sign of improvement despite the strenuous efforts of sympathetic Western governments and a host of international relief agencies; the roads were if anything still worse, there was still no postal or telephone service, health provision had not improved, and the chronic power cuts were demoralizing people and causing unrest. And there was still a civil war, one of the longest and most destructive, going on in the eastern part of the country, with neighboring powers supporting the rebels and jostling for influence over the immensely valuable natural resources waiting to be exploited in the region. But, however unstable the country, the immediate challenge of helping street children was as urgent as ever, and we continued our efforts to get the children's home started.

During our second visit we had been greatly helped by the British ambassador, who gave us a lunch to meet people from other NGOs and promised his support. His wife also became an active agent for us, and it was she who first sounded an alarm. Despite assurances that Raphaël had given us several times, it transpired through her inquiries that the house and compound still did not belong to us. A very experienced Swiss lady who had been working in the DRC for many years helped us to pursue this; and it turned out that the property did not belong to Raphaël at all, but to his sister. We then insisted that they should immediately get this rectified, so that our charity would become the owners; but we were met with systematic prevarication. We employed a lawyer to formalize the transaction; but even though he met and negotiated with the parties he failed to get them to sign.

At this point Raphaël disappeared, and we never heard from him again. We had spent all our donors' money on re-furbishing the house, as well as on Raphaël's travel and living expenses, and the result was merely to have greatly improved a house belonging to his family without any assurance of benefiting anyone but them. For some months I went on trying to make contact with Raphaël through a close friend of his in Kinshasa who ran a human rights organization and whom we had come to trust. This friend professed himself to be equally dismayed, and was, I think, genuinely puzzled by Raphaël's behavior — not least because Raphaël still had his wife and young son living in London and a return ticket to come home. But it was years before anything was heard of him, and then it was no more than an appeal for money made to someone who had worked with him at the church in Leicester Square. Consequently I gave up hope of salvaging anything of the project and dissolved the charity.

As well as having been a disastrous venture in the world of charitable work abroad, it was a shock to me personally. I had known Raphaël for about ten years, and had come to think of him as a friend as well as a gifted, imaginative, and generous organizer. Admittedly there were things that had puzzled us for many months. Though we invited them several times, we were never introduced to his wife and small son. I had met her briefly before they were married: she was also an asylum seeker from Kinshasa and David Alton had helped her to get leave to remain; indeed he attended their wedding and was struck by the respect with which his neighbors and friends evidently regarded Raphaël. Yet his family life remained a mystery to us; we simply had to assume that African ways were different from ours. And there were also some practical matters over which we found him evasive. Yet we were all experienced people, and we all had confidence in him. I then had to face the question: Had he been deceiving us all along? Had someone to whom I had given my friendship and on whose behalf I had dedicated a great deal of effort been playing a trick on us? It seemed unlikely; and yet when I looked back over the controls we had sought to exercise over his conduct in the project, I could see that there were many occasions when we should have been stricter and could have been exploited. In the end I formed the judgment that he was not deliberately deceiving us. He certainly had an ambition for the Jedidiah Foundation (he had chosen this Old Testament name for both his son and for the charity) to be able to exert some influence for good in Kinshasa, but he had run up against the strong African tradition that family property was sacred and must not ever be parted with. He may have hoped, naïvely, that the project could go ahead without this ever having to be resolved; but when it became clear that we were determined to see it through on a legal basis, he could not face confessing the truth to us and simply disappeared. It seemed then that I, along with my thoroughly experienced committee, had allowed ourselves to be led up the path and wasted the large amount of money given to us by well-wishers.

I was chairman, and had ultimate responsibility for the fiasco. Should I feel ashamed? Of course; here was another field in which I had shown myself to be an amateur, and I should not have been meddling with such things. But a wise friend gave me some reassurance: it is always better, he said, to trust someone even when that trust is betrayed, than to withhold trust when it would have been deserved. And after all, it did give me an experience I had yearned for, a brief acquaintance with black Africa. After my return I read up the history of the appalling regime and the cruelties imposed by King Leopold on his colony, then called the Congo Free State (which he was eventually forced to sell to the Belgian government in 1905). This was the subject of the searing report made to the British government in 1904 by the consul, Roger Casement, after several months' journeying through the country, and had also been vividly described in Conrad's *Heart of*

Darkness. It seemed that the Belgian administration that followed, though less obviously inhumane, did little to reduce the exploitation, and when Independence came there was no more than a handful of men to administer the country who had received any higher education — only the religious orders had provided serious schooling. But one gift the Belgians did bring was the French language. This had flourished, and I was constantly amazed by what I heard. The better educated Africans conversed with a precision and elegance that would put to shame what passes for normal conversation and even formal reporting in England.

Perhaps this judgment shows a certain partiality. French is the one language in which I have become really fluent, and I continue to experience a slight feeling of liberation when I speak it. For the last few years Julian and I have spent our summer holiday as guests in a convent in south Brittany. It seems not widely known that French religious houses offer hospitality to holiday makers each summer (there is even a substantial directory available of those which do so) and apart from a minimum of respect for the life and rhythm of the communities who run them, the guests are left entirely free to enjoy their stay in any way they wish. This particular convent at St. Gildas de Rhuys in south Brittany is attached to the fine abbey church that was built in the twelfth century, and the original monastery received (and attempted to poison) Peter Abelard when he was exiled from Paris. In those days the country was wild and uncivilized; its coast is now a magnet for summer visitors and has evolved accordingly. The monastery, having been ruined in the French Revolution, was rebuilt in the nineteenth century as a house for female religious working for destitute girls. It still belongs to the same order, and half a dozen nuns live there supervising the running of a house which will accommodate up to a hundred guests for conferences, retreats or (in the summer) simple holidays by the sea. We found it by accident long before we left Westminster, and soon made it a regular destination each summer. One of its charms was the social life among the visitors. At each meal we found ourselves sitting next to French priests, monks, nuns, and lay folk who again and again turned out to be persons of great interest; many of them became friends. In our very first visit we sat next to an elderly nun who was telling stories. An old woman's stories, I thought, were the last thing I wanted to hear; but suddenly my attention was held. The subtlety and humor of these ones was arresting. She was called Soeur Monique, and remained a close friend right until her death. She had contributed regularly to the local religious radio programs, and even interviewed me for them; and I was not surprised. She spoke the most clear, cultured, and precise French of anyone I have met, and with this she had a gift of story-telling that made her conversation a continual delight. At the same time her physical sufferings were often intense, though seldom mentioned. She had received treatment for cancer years before, which had been mal-administered and left her permanently lame, and with her right arm and hand paralyzed. One of the reasons for our return to the convent each summer was to be able to continue our conversations with her. And each time we would also have new experiences and make new friends.

None of the nuns wears a religious habit of any kind, and the French church life that I experienced there, as on most of my visits to France since the 1960s, was the direct consequence of the Second Vatican Council. The old rigidities had disappeared, the openness to non-Catholic denominations was almost invariable, and the vivacious informality of worship, though still conducted within official guidelines, was often an inspiration for those, like me, who had become impatient with the conservative tendencies of their own churches. Again and again I met priests of that generation who welcomed me as a brother in the faith and opened up possibilities in pastoral practice and spirituality that I had not seen before. It was because of this that I had taken parties of my students to France to open their minds to a different style of ministry; and because the guests who came to this convent were mainly older men and women, I continued to be nourished by the same innovative tradition long after I retired. Meanwhile younger priests were following a different path: their church, like much of ours, was retreating to old ways and old certainties, and we had little in common on the rare occasions I met them. But I could still look forward to our annual visit to Brittany as a time to be refreshed by priests and religious visitors who represented something of the sense of springtime and adventure that had transformed the church in France in the years following the Council. There were of course also less serious reasons for going. The convent was in view of the sea, on a gorgeous coast line with splendid beaches; and Julian was inspired to paint some of her best pictures there.

We were indeed fortunate to have formed this connection. As Julian's condition worsened no other foreign travel was possible: everything had to be familiar and predictable. I could be quite sure of every detail of a journey we had done many times and of the sensitive welcome we would receive when we arrived. Julian was no longer able to carry on normal conversations even in English; the fact that everything was in French was in a way an advantage, because people could assume she understood nothing and they politely accepted her silence. For me, on the other hand, it was an annual opportunity to indulge my love of things French and my pleasure in speaking the language; and this annual refreshment more than made up for the restrictions that Julian's dementia was imposing on our life at home. When Julian's condition reached a stage where even this journey became impossible, I had to rely entirely on my own inner resources to sustain both me and her (she died in 2015). It is to these that I shall devote a final chapter.

CHAPTER 9

A Christian Stoic?

I suppose the first real test of these resources was Julian's illness
that set in while we were still in Oxford in 1981. At the beginning, it
seemed like a crisis that would pass when the hospital treatment had
done its work. But the initial spell in the Warneford hospital was prolonged for many weeks and soon became a trial for all the family; for
me and Victoria (who, aged only twelve, was with me throughout) it
was a searing experience. When a serious illness is physical it evokes
deep reserves of empathy and compassion in those close to the sufferer; but an acute affliction of the mind is different. The spectacle of
Julian seeming, in a sense, hardly the same person, apparently impervious to all words of consolation or encouragement, and subjected to
the inhumane regime of the hospital, caused in us a deeper emotional
turmoil. But when the acute phase had passed, an apparent cure was
found in a single daily dose of lithium — not so much a drug, as a
chemical substance making good a physical deficiency; and the subsequent recurrences were all quite short-lived — a matter of weeks
rather than months. What then took their place was a pattern of life
dominated by what used to be called manic depression, now bi-polar
disorder. Not that in this case it was ever truly bi-polar: the periods of
clinical depression could be acute, but they were never matched by
a comparable manic phase. When Julian emerged from them, life returned to normality, with only occasional symptoms of serious over-
excitement. These times of normality could last for many months —
there was once a family celebration when one had lasted for a whole

year. But more often they lasted for only two or three months. Like so many psychiatric patients, after a spell of good health Julian would begin to feel she could manage without her pills, and either openly or (if she knew we were concerned) secretly give up taking them. The result, invariably, was a renewed onset of depression, which would last about six weeks (presuming she went back to her medication); and these episodes took place two or three times a year for the next twenty-five years, often coinciding with family occasions such as our daughters' weddings, and very often also dampening our festivities at Christmas or on anniversaries.

It was difficult for other members of the family not to feel a certain bitterness that so much was being cast into shadow by something that (they naturally felt) could have been avoided if Julian had shown more will to do so; but one factor in her condition was a consistent state of denial. When she was well, she was apparently incapable of recognizing that anything had been wrong with her; and this made it at times almost impossible to persuade her to take her daily dose. I could not find it in myself to blame her for this. It was evidently a part of her self-defense, a way of combating the terrible lack of self-confidence that followed each attack. And the fact that she seemed unaware of the darkness and misery that both she and we had been undergoing could be seen as a merciful form of amnesia; otherwise memories of it might have haunted her for the rest of her life. The result, inevitably, was a certain estrangement from the family, who all made valiant efforts to maintain their affection, loyalty, and indeed their support for me, but could not continue in a relaxed and close relationship with their mother. For me, who was with her for many hours each day, the burden was taxing, especially during my time at the Abbey, when official duties had somehow to be carried out without leaving her too long alone or exposing her to situations she could not cope with.

Yet it would be wrong to assume from this apparent amnesia that the causes of her depressions lay entirely in her physical and psychological condition. My own failure to adapt myself sufficiently to her deeper needs and to enter into her private world may have been a factor that brought them on — a thought that has caused me much distress. One of her poems gives more than a hint of this. It was written during a night in Westminster, and evidently addressed to me (though she never showed it to me):

> If we could have worked together,
> How wonderful it would have been,
> Tuned into that sphere for ever,
> Kept silence for the world unseen.
>
> Then each from our essential space,
> Each listening self unharmed by noise,
> Could plot our route, our pilgrim race,
> Gifted now with separate poise.
>
> Then both, midst work and family,
> (Sufficient time to hear alone)
> Would with new sight forge unity,
> A highway straight — and no bruised bone....
>
> Each of us, humble to pooled sight,
> Fostered by still attempts at prayer,
> Would then re-trim our fancy's flight,
> And different revelations dare.

Another recurring theme in her poems, directed against the exigencies of our life more than against any failure of mine, was her sense of enforced separation from the world of nature, of her spiritual freedom being lost amid the necessary routines (which she called "housen-cares") of family and social life. I have already mentioned that her apparent indifference to the details of religious observance belied a deep spiritual life, which made her long to withdraw at times from the pressures of the daily domestic routine. It was certainly nourished by the periods of time she was able to spend painting or writing; but she needed longer periods of quiet and solitude. We found a place for this early in our married life. It was a house called St. Julian's (pure coincidence!) in Sussex, founded by Florence Allshorn, a retired missionary. She had become convinced that when missionaries came home on furlough, it was quite wrong for them to be sent relentlessly round the country to give talks about their work. They needed rest and refreshment, and for this purpose she gathered a small group of like-minded women to form a lay community, with provisional vows and commitment, to make such a venture possible. They acquired a large house in Sussex with beautiful grounds and a lake where herons came to nest, and opened their doors to any whose work involved pastoral responsibility — missionaries, clergy, social workers, and others. The regime was designed for maximum tranquility without any imposed restraint, other than silence at the graciously served meals. Breakfast was brought to the bedrooms, there was a log fire burning in the sitting room, there was a large and varied library (by no means all devotional books), and opportunity for solitude or society as preferred. Julian and I went there first together; but I soon began to feel that it was her special place, and encouraged her to go alone; indeed one visit that I made with her was not a success, as I tried to describe in a poem of my own (an exercise in the ancient Greek meter of *ionics a minore*: $\smile\smile - -$).

> Once you came here — to a rest-place
> For your tired limbs, to a home-place
> For your dulled mind, to the healing
> And the quietness that you longed for,
> As the heron drops to the island.
> But your rest-place had a void place,
> For your tired self was a half-self
> As your soul grew in aloneness,
> So your love ran to your mind's plan
> To enlist me in your praising.
> So I came then to your rest-place
> And my praises grew alongside
> Inattentive to your mind's plan.
> Do our loved ones fit in templates
> Which the mind shapes in a void place?

No, our souls change as our love runs
And the banks yield to the strong flow
Of a stream bent to a new land.
So unbounded is our praising
As the heron drops to its home-place.

Thus I learned to respect her spiritual needs, but never was able to adapt myself fully to them or penetrate into the experience that prompted them. She would never talk about them to me, and I learned most about them from her poetry, which I often typed for her. Here is another poem that reflects a painful recollection of having her deepest instincts misunderstood.

Mist of winter, whose closed shoots
Can give a sheen of muted red
Through dark cowls — but all crave roots
As mice and cats seek sleep in bed.

Could I protect myself this way
Impervious in winter dress?
Feel anchored in His world, His clay,
Miming wind and rain without stress?

Here He intended us to be
With Dryad siblings and the rest,
And here alone my spirit's free:
Drugs? Counsel? No! Creation — blessed!

Let us now dance with the trees.
Then I will put ear to the ground,
Await the breath of sleeping bee
Which may take long to turn to sound.

After my retirement, the pattern of Julian's depressions continued unchanged for nearly ten years, apart from one acute one which entailed a short spell of in-patient treatment in a local hospital. Here the regime was utterly different from what she had endured twenty years previously. The staff were humane and caring, the environment civilized and relatively unregulated, and when Julian was discharged, the depression having lifted, she was seen bidding patients and staff quite warm farewells. But at the end of 2007 something more serious made its appearance. Once more her depression became acute and unmanageable at home, and she was taken back to the same hospital. This time, the consultants believed, the cause was different. She had begun to show signs of dementia (the GP had warned of this) and the consultants thought that a different course of treatment should be followed. This was entirely unsuccessful, and no improvement was seen for over two months. Only when they were persuaded to restore the usual dose of lithium did the depression lift; but by then Julian had spent three months in the ward and the experience had become difficult to endure. After that, however, there were no more recurrences of the depression (and, strangely, no resistance to her regular dosage) but the diagnosis of incipient dementia turned out to be correct, and the illness gathered pace until, in 2012, there was no alternative to a care home: I was simply unable to make her happy at home, quite apart from the increasing difficulty of physical care. It was an immense relief to find that under the excellent and very personal care of a specially trained staff in a care home dedicated to dementia, she became contented to a degree that had seemed impossible when I was caring for her single-handed.

How did I cope with the strain? I had a great deal of sympathy and support, and colleagues at the Abbey were sensitive enough to ease the embarrassments that our inevitable contacts with the world outside our home would precipitate (in this respect things became much easier when we retired and life could be more private and secluded). But I was also becoming aware of a trait in my character that was crucial. People might assume that my ultimate support was my Christian faith; but in reality it had more to do with a rigid stoicism that had become part of my make-up and which, allied with continual good health, enabled me to persevere without seriously wavering. I doubt if this was a conscious philosophy. True, I had taught my Oxford students about the Stoics, and in theory I knew quite a lot about

Stoic philosophy; but it was only much later that I came to see that
their contribution was not so much a philosophical system (which
had been the focus of my interest and teaching) as the inculcation
of a way of life, enabling its adherents to sustain the manifold mis-
fortunes to which all human beings are vulnerable — in the ancient
world they were especially so: the average age of death was not more
than forty. So long as my Christian faith remained strong, I could believe that my stoic abilities were God-given and God-strengthened;
but during my last years at Westminster I began to experience what
at the time I took to be a form of the "Dark Night of the Soul": I found
an exact description of my feelings in St. John of the Cross's book of
this name, except that I did not have something that is fundamental to his analysis, a continued yearning for the God who seemed so
unaccountably absent; I was not "yearning" for him at all, but simply
getting used to doing without him. But later I had to recognize that
this was a real waning of my faith, and that my stoicism was simply
part of my make-up, for which indeed I am grateful, but which seems
independent of any faith in God. Does this mean that my true religion has always been stoicism, not Christianity?

In part, I think, yes. In recent years I have come to feel a certain
liberation in abandoning some of the traditional Christian disciplines
that I have had difficulties with all my life, such as the acknowledge-
ment of universal sinfulness and the need for constant penitence: if I
now join in confessions of sin, it is for me more a matter of acknowl-
edging the lamentable state of the world and the responsibility of
human beings (like myself) for letting it drift so far from what must
have been the intentions of the creator. My own "sins," that I am indeed conscious of, are better described as failures of good sense and
a lack of sensitivity, which can best be dealt with by exercising self-
discipline rather than by seeking personal forgiveness from God. On
the other hand, stoicism in its classical form, though it encouraged altruistic behavior in the interests of the common good, was altogether
lacking in the notion of service to the weak and vulnerable, which is
at the heart of the Christian ethic and which continues to challenge
and inspire me. My reliance on a stoic resilience had not amounted to
a total abandonment of the Christian faith — at least, not at that stage.

What were Julian's own feelings during this time? It was exceedingly hard to tell. The consistent denial she had shown with regard to her depression continued when her main symptoms became the confusion and memory loss that go with dementia. She would never recognize that anything had changed, and there was no way of explaining her condition to her or helping her to come to terms with it. As with her denial of depression, this may have been a merciful protection from the devastating symptoms of her illness; but what was happening to her confidence in herself, her religious faith, and her perception of the world around her was impossible to tell. As time passed she seemed unable even to recognize the pictures she had painted or the prose and poetry she had written; it was as if whole segments of her personality were disappearing, and no foothold was left for any mutual exploration or sharing. For me, it was indeed an early bereavement. What it was for her remained inscrutable.

The next real test of my resources was the death of our third daughter Christian in 2008. Christian was perhaps the most obviously talented and creative of our four children. After gaining a place to read classics at Oxford she went to Paris to work as an *au pair* and to attend the mime school of her choice; indeed she scoured Paris and visited them all to make sure she would be taught what she really wanted to learn, *mime corporelle*. She then went to my own Oxford college (Worcester) for the four-year "Greats" course, after which she returned to Paris with a French government scholarship for two more years of intensive mime study, supporting herself by teaching English. This, in turn, was followed by a year in Siena, teaching English at the university and (in her own estimation) completing her education by adding some Italian to her knowledge of languages. When she returned to London she adopted a new stage name (Christian Darley, after my maternal grandmother), and proved herself to be an outstanding mime artist in a number of performances, some of which were astoundingly beautiful; they were mainly in quite small theaters, but on two occasions, to my delight, she performed in Westminster Abbey. In due course she took a post as teacher of movement in the London Academy of Music and Dramatic Arts (LAMDA), where she met a brilliant musician, Anthony Ingle. They got married, and their daughter Joy was born in 1998. But not long after, she developed cancer of the breast, and was operated on in 2000. This was successful, in that there was a remission and she was able to return to work for several years and move the family home from Catford in London to Sherborne in Dorset. But the cancer returned, this time in an invasive form, against which she battled using every resource known, from spiritual healing to diet and herbal medicine, alongside the medical treatments to which she submitted only after careful and critical examination of their success rates and likely efficacity. The struggle continued until she finally succumbed in May 2008, leaving a daughter of ten years old. But in the months before she died she succeeded in writing a book about her teaching methods that was edited by three of her friends and was published shortly after her death (*The Space to Move*, 2009). It is an enthralling read. Her classical education had given her an enviable facility for a lucid and elegant style of writing, and the book reveals much of her sparkling personality and her extraordinary talent. It also shows the influence on her of the French mime school she followed, and the creative originality with which she handled it. Her death at the age of forty-six was felt to be a tragedy far outside the circle of her family and close friends.

It happened that it was during the last six months of her life, when she was already virtually confined to bed and in constant pain (she had the misfortune to be allergic to all effective pain killers) that Julian's last severe depression resulted in the three months' stay in hospital that I mentioned earlier. This, though acutely disturbing for me, also enabled me to see far more of Christian than I had been able to do for many years. I could visit Julian in the morning, take an afternoon train to Sherborne and be in time to spend the evening and part of the next morning at Christian's bedside before taking the train back and seeing Julian in the late afternoon. These visits to Christian had a practical motive. There were times when her husband had to be in London for his professional work, and there were difficulties in finding a nurse to take his place for the night. So I was able, about once a week over a period of two or three months, to step in and do simple things for her like giving her supper and hot drinks when she needed them during the night. But the reward — for both of us, it seemed — was the creation of an intimacy we never had before. Christian loved to talk, loved the opportunities talking gives to explore shared experiences and reactions, and when we looked back together over some of her most vivid memories — always enlivened by her humorous characterizations of those who peopled them — our conversations reached a level of intimacy that I had seldom experienced. Indeed she told one of her sisters that "it had almost been worth getting ill to get to know my father so well."

It was indeed a precious experience, and I fully accept the implied reproof. This was the first time I had been confided in at this depth by any of my children. When they were small, I was probably quite a good father, sharing their games and leading them into adventures. But the inevitable strains of adolescence, and the estrangements that resulted from them, created barriers that I had never fully overcome. And I have to say that their mother's role in the family did not make it easier. She had given them an exceptionally rich and creative childhood. Her imaginative story-telling, her spontaneity, and her many-sided creativity made them endlessly resourceful in their shared occupations. At the same time it developed in them a sensitivity to the feelings and needs of others that made all of them into a model of care and hospitality for strangers. But as they grew into adults Julian seemed to have little sense of allowing them to develop their own independence and characters. So far as I can tell from her recollections and diaries, she seems never to have rebelled from her parents or ceased to enjoy an exceptionally easy and frank relationship with them. By the time I knew her in Florence they were a closely-bonded family unit. But this, unfortunately, did not prepare her for the need of her own children to explore the world on their own terms. One consequence of this was that on the many occasions when she sought to dictate their conduct and openly criticized their attitudes and their preferences, I found myself torn between my natural solidarity with her and my instinct that they must be allowed their freedom. Again and again I would try to persuade her, but, having failed, I had to ally myself with her. The result, naturally, was to increase the estrangement from my children, and I doubt if I had ever felt entirely at ease with any of them as adults until these moments of effortless intimacy with Christian in the last months of her life.

Christian's death came just a week after a party that she organized from her bed for Joy's tenth birthday. She had willed herself, against all the odds, to remain alive to see it, and allowed all the children to come to her bedside at the end for what Joy, at least, sensed was a farewell. Joy then went off to stay with her closest friend, and did not come back for the final days, evidently feeling that she had taken leave of her mother at the best moment. When her father told her that she had died, she sat on his knee and sobbed for five minutes, and then went back to her game with her friend, which was doubtless the best way a ten-year-old child could have reacted. The rest of us — that is to say Christian's husband, two sisters, and myself — watched by Christian's bedside in her own home and had the privilege of accompanying her as her life was being overtaken by the mystery of death. Our eldest daughter, Marina (who lived in New Zealand), had said her farewells on a visit to England a few months previously and sensibly decided not to come again; and Julian, whose state of mind could barely cope with the reality of death, was providentially cared for by an old friend of the family not many miles away, allowing me to join the others during the last hours of Christian's life. She died in her husband's arms with her closest family beside her.

Characteristically, she had given careful thought, during her many months of illness, to the form of her funeral. It was to be at Cerne Abbas, a church she had come to love, and that has an exceptionally beautiful graveyard. The service was to be a celebration of her life as well as a solemn leave-taking. Joy was to be there, as were half a dozen other children of her age, all friends, whose mothers took them out of school for the occasion. Anthony, the musician, both played some of the music and gave a brief testimony to her exceptional gifts and character; but the surprise came when the Franciscan from Hilfield Friary, who had been visiting her regularly and become a close confidant, read a letter that she had written to be read out to us during the service. The impact on us all was extraordinary: it was as if she were present with us, revealing a strength of character such as we could have barely imagined. The letter had a wide circulation afterwards, even being quoted in full by a rabbi friend in his sermon on the eve of the Day of Atonement. It fully deserves being printed here.

From Christian
read at her Funeral by Br Raymond Christian SSF

It isn't perhaps conventional for the person who died to make a speech, but the performer in me cannot resist a final few words in front of an audience of a very special kind.

My beloved husband, my beloved daughter, my beloved parents, my beloved sisters and their partners, my oh so beloved and extraordinary friends — I am glad you are here. I have had a full life, an exciting one: one full of movement and colour, from an expedition to Jerusalem aged four, to my time in Oxford, Paris, Italy, London and Sherborne. Every encounter has been precious and made my life rich. A life full of golden moments beyond measure.

My life brimmed with such richness on meeting Anthony, a man who has held me, loved me and made me laugh. He told me, not long into this illness, that he'd married someone "on a journey": he never ceased to hold my hand on that journey and steered me through the roughest patches. When, after our marriage, I felt I had no room for any more delicious love, Joy was born. My Joy, Joy, Joy, Joy. Watching her grow and become her own person has been my greatest privilege, and with Anthony, the love that surrounds her is boundless, yet it was they who taught me that love could be such.

My family and friends: if illness can be sometimes a gift, which sometimes slightly annoying New Age people say it is, then the gift it has given me is Love. This is no cliché: I have felt held, supported and cherished by you all in your wonderful and extraordinary different ways. Love and friendship cannot die, so thanks to you I feel happily immortal. All of you have thoroughly formed my life and I thank you for being the marvellous people you are. Grieve a bit but not too much, because as Odysseus said (and my goodness he knew about grieving

and endurance!) the "belly gets hungry and needs to be fed." So
I urge you in the spirit of the Classics to eat, drink and, please,
celebrate my life with Joy. . . .

My life has been sprinkled with grains of gold — it has
been rich and it has been precious — because of all of you.

Enough! Sing, eat, be merry. My biggest regret is not having enough time to talk — please do it for me.

Sure enough, we all went to the village hall afterwards, where the
children let off steam with rumbustious games, food and drink were
shared, and where it seemed entirely appropriate for there to be a
large birthday cake for Victoria, whose birthday was on the same day.

How did we all react in the longer term? Anthony, who adored
Christian, was visibly affected, yet had played one of the two pianos
in the last movement of Milhaud's *Scaramouche* at the end of the service — "the most triumphant piece I know." He was evidently conscious of the way in which Christian's heroic struggle against cancer
seemed in the end to have been a victory of the spirit over the flesh.
His sense of bereavement had, of course, begun earlier: Christian's
long spell of almost perpetual pain had drastically affected their life
together; but he seemed to have the resources needed to resume
his normal life and occupations. Her sisters felt the loss acutely. She
had been the most vivid and creative member of the family, and her
departure from it caused them pangs for many months. It also burdened Helen, our second daughter, with the responsibility — which
she gladly accepted — for giving Joy a secure second home on the
many occasions that her father had to be away to follow his career as
a musician and teacher in London. Helen has no children of her own,
but is immensely gifted with them and has been able to give to Joy
much of the parental love and care that she lost through her mother's
death. Indeed she had been preparing for this ever since she moved
from the north-east to a village quite close to Sherborne, Christian's
home, so as to be close to her sister in her last months.

For Julian, it was hard to say what she felt. When I took her to
the house a few hours after Christian died, she was fully aware of
the dead body in front of her, but remained dry-eyed; and her atti-

tude of denial in the face of hard reality made her comment afterwards that the Franciscan, when he performed the committal at the graveside, "obviously felt that it was all quite wrong." In her mind the funeral had been some kind of ugly mistake, and for months she would express surprise whenever we reminded her that Christian was no longer alive. Dementia, it seems, can enhance previous traits of character; and her denial of unwelcome eventualities had begun to affect her ability to recognize even the fact of mortality.

For myself, I have long reflected on the effect it had on me. In the graveyard I was tearful (as were others) to a degree I was not prepared for, and for a while afterwards tears would come unbidden as memories surfaced. The last few months of hitherto unknown intimacy with Christian had done something to lessen the slight awkwardness and diffidence which I still felt with my children, and I sensed there was more emotional charge to be released in me than in any previous family event. But at the same time the distance and objectivity I had cultivated in pastoral relationships made it easier for me to stand back and think of this as just another death, evoking both my own stoicism and my professional ability to be the consoler rather than the consoled. Even though the emotional turmoil had been quite severe at the time, I found I very soon reverted to what must have seemed to others a dismayingly dispassionate manner of reacting to the loss of such a gifted and deeply loved daughter.

The third and most fundamental test of my resources has been the fluctuation and eventual erosion of my faith. From the start it had always been subject to doubts and difficulties, though there had also been periods of relative serenity and confidence. The initial challenge, at theological college, was to discern whether I was truly called to be a priest. In the end I gained sufficient confidence to go forward, though not without recurrent uncertainties; and my resolve may have been strengthened by certain moments of what seemed like authentic religious experience — one of them was even felt simultaneously by Julian when we visited a numinous church together. But I also found an affinity in myself with the situation described by Graham Greene in his play, *The Potting Shed*, which I had seen when it was first staged in London in 1958. It is the story of a determinedly atheist family whose son (as we learn at the end of the play) had hanged himself in the potting shed at the end of the garden at the age of fourteen and had been found dead by the gardener. His uncle, who had become a Roman Catholic priest (in defiance of his atheist brother), had taken the dead boy in his arms and, by a supreme effort of prayer, had brought him back to life. He then lost his faith and became a typical Graham Greene whisky priest, keeping up the appearance of his clerical duties but carrying them out (when sober) entirely without conviction. West End audiences were puzzled, if not frankly uncomprehending. How could someone who had apparently performed a miracle through faith and prayer not have his faith strengthened? How could he possibly have lost it afterwards? But I found this easily comprehensible and true to life. Religious experiences can be very powerful at the time; the problem is (or may be) to sustain their effect in the years that follow. As the experience recedes in memory, so the question of its authenticity raises more doubts than certainties; and when I look back at the moments when it seemed that the transcendent was impinging directly upon me, I find it all too easy to think in terms of psychological auto-suggestion — and anyway (as I have come to think), if God is truly the unimaginably powerful and purposeful creator of the whole universe, is it plausible that a personal intervention of this kind could derive from such a being or could be anything other than a projection of my own expectations, nourished by centuries of anecdotal testimony, but surely at an impossible distance from the immense and mysterious reality that is God?

But if I could not draw strength from these memories, I could certainly continue my search for spiritual reassurance. I made regular short retreats in convents and monasteries (the Anglican Benedictine nuns at West Malling were particularly welcoming and restorative) and often felt a sense of serenity and hopefulness that I could believe was the result of probing and refreshing my faith. But though I continued this pattern faithfully until Julian's continual need of me made it impossible, I found the expected strengthening less and less evident, and even the beauty and prayerfulness of the place, which had never failed to revive my spirit, began to lose its power. The amount of the Christian faith that I could truly assent to was diminishing all the time; and the search for any kind of religious experience had come to seem like the quest for satisfying a human need rather than for a serious encounter with a God who must surely not be directly associated with such moments of psychological reassurance. These uncertainties slowly grew into a kind of spiritual numbness, into a disinclination even to explore the question whether I still believed in God; but I received the helpful advice that much of this was due simply to the diversion of almost all my thoughts and cares to the needs of Julian, and to the exhaustion of my spiritual energies. It would take years, I was told — and who knows if I would be allotted them? — before I would have the spiritual energy once more to take serious stock of myself and my beliefs; meanwhile I must be content to let things slide.

This raised the question, of course, whether it was proper and honest for me to go on behaving like a priest and leading others in worship. Was I merely mouthing religious formulae without finding meaning in them myself? Would it not be more honest to declare my slippage from faith and leave priestly tasks to others? And I had similar doubts about other activities that went with being a priest. I was often told that I had a talent for making the Bible come alive, and my expositions and lectures were eagerly attended. But sometimes I had to ask myself whether this gift was anything to do with a belief in Scripture's inspiration. Could I perhaps have done just as well if I were guiding people through Shakespeare? Didn't I have much the same effect when I lectured about ancient sites on Hellenic cruises? And again, when I did pastoral work and tried to bring strength and consolation to those in trouble, I sensed that I was becoming adept at saying the right words at the right time; but whether they were backed by enough conviction to give any real help, and whether the professional distance from sufferers, which I had deliberately cultivated, was merely making me insensitive to the depth of their suffering, sometimes surfaced as nagging questions.

And I had a further scruple. If my fundamental motivation has been the sense of fulfilment that comes from service to others, how genuine is it? Just as biologists in their study of the animal kingdom constantly seek to find other explanations of apparently altruistic behavior, so too I examined my instinct to serve others as a possible cover for some darker and more self-centered interest. Christian witness, for example, as we were warned by Jesus, is liable to result in abuse, humiliation, even persecution and death — as I was poignantly reminded when I was working on the Westminster Abbey martyrs project. But have I, as a minister utterly committed to this witness by my ordination vows, ever been exposed to any of this? When "serving" as a priest, whether functioning in church or consoling as a counsellor, have I been insulated by my liturgical role and clerical status — even by my clerical dress — from the cynical view, held by many, of the religion I profess? When I hand out cups of tea to the homeless at a day center, I take refuge behind the activity of serving and so avoid any deep encounter with the realities with which the victim is wrestling. In this still predominantly Christian country the social acceptance of religion and religions enables ministers, apart from a few bold and adventurous ones, to live and work without the threat of public mockery or obloquy.

This was brought home to me one day when I ventured outside the privileged precincts of Westminster Abbey in my church uniform of a red cassock. I was on my way to a Buckingham Palace Garden party, where we were invited to wear cassocks, otherwise it would never have occurred to me to appear like this in public (I was going to the palace on foot). I was greeted by a jeering group of young people: "Here comes Danny La Rue" — the best known transvestite performer at the time. The other side of this was a visit I paid some forty years ago to one of the L'Arche houses for mentally disabled people. This one was run by the sister of Jean Vanier, the founder, and was not far from Canterbury. When I arrived I was instantly greeted by one of the residents, who wanted to know my Christian name (less casually used in those days than it is now). My experience I found well described by Henri Nouwen, the well-known spiritual writer, who spent the last years of his life in one of these houses. It is an environment where nothing has any significance save the sort of person one is. Accustomed to introducing himself as a writer, an academic, in short a man of note, he found himself, as I did, with nothing whatever to say that would mean anything to the residents other than what would show that he was ready to be their friend. And so it was with me, making me abruptly conscious of the extent to which I am normally protected from the need of any such self-exposure by the privileged social class and professional environment in which I have lived. Along with this experience goes my attachment to Taizé, which seems to owe its astonishing attraction for young people to the simple fact that there is no sign of privilege or protection of any kind distancing the Brothers from those with whom they come in contact. It is these experiences that have occasionally brought to the surface a deep yearning to form relationships with others at this basic level of the meeting of naked, unprotected souls. To know God, the mystics have often said, you must first know yourself. I suspect it is this lack of knowledge, and so of confidence in myself, which has always caused in me a certain unease in the presence of all but those who could never pose a threat — children, the elderly, the dependent — and which perhaps is a factor that continues to deprive me of any secure conviction of the existence of God, such as would be expected of any minister of religion.

In recent years similar doubts have come into my mind about other aspects of my ministry. One of the fundamental tasks and duties of a Christian minister is to bring others to Christ. Looking back, I wonder if I have ever succeeded in doing so. Indeed I am not sure that I ever really tried. And the reason, I believe, must be that I was never sufficiently confident in my own faith to wish to pass it on to others. I did, of course, devote a great deal of intellectual study to it, and became a competent theologian. But this does not mean that, at a deep level, I was convinced of the truth of theological propositions. It is possible to think of theology as a kind of grammar. The propositions it asserts need to be logically related to one another and understood in their proper order and relationships. The church, for instance, uses the formula of the Trinity comprising the Father who created us, the Son who redeems us, and the Holy Spirit who sanctifies us. To get these terms in the wrong order — to say, for instance, that the Son created us and the Father redeems us — would not necessarily make them untrue or meaningless, but it would offend against theological grammar; and it is arguable that the whole edifice of Christian doctrine represents an effort (often brilliantly accomplished by brilliant minds) to assemble such propositions in a logically coherent order that is also consonant with the data offered by Scripture. But to know the grammar of a language is not to have evidence that the language itself relates to any reality. It is quite possible to perfect the use of it without checking whether it refers to anything in the real world.

In 2008 I found a disturbing expression of this possibility in a novel of Charles Williams that I happened to be reading to Julian. I recorded the impact it made on me in my diary:

> "They probably liked their religion taken mild — a pious hope, a devout ejaculation, a general sympathetic sense of a kindly universe. . . ."

These words describe exactly what I have come to feel religion to be — pious, devout, generally sympathetic, and optimistic. Williams, of course, is contrasting it with agony, bewilderment, uncreated light, a much more powerful and awesome reality; hence it is "mild." That's not how I see it. Religion, with these components, need not be "mild" at all. It gives strength and depth to living — and dying. It can also, of course, turn vicious and violent. But that is not the question, which is whether the immense edifice of theology and spirituality which is built upon these admirable and necessary foundations expresses any reality beyond itself. The more definite, dogmatic, and detailed religious language becomes, the less it seems to me that it could possibly relate to a reality which we could seriously call God.

Unless, in some way, it does. Of Damaris, a blinkered young aspiring scholar, Charles Williams makes her lover say,

> ". . . she would go on thoughtfully playing with the dead pictures of ideas, with names and philosophies, Plato and Pythagoras and Anselm and Abelard, Athens and Alexandria and Paris, Gnostic traditions, medieval rituals, Angels and Archangels — they were cards she was playing in her own game. But she didn't know, she didn't understand."

What if the reality behind the cards of my theology that I have been playing with all my life were to break through my stoic carapace? But it's hard to see what tools it could use to do so beyond what has already been tried — Christian's dying and death, an increasing sense of bereavement from Julian with her dementia, the wretchedness for both of us in her depressions, and a sense that aging, though amazingly deferred in my case, was making preliminary advances on me (slight deafness, and incipient arthritis in my hands affecting violin playing and handwriting). And far from being able to tune myself to any possible revelation or moment of faith, I found myself saying, with Yellow Dog Dingo (for I was responsible for there being any), "What's for breakfast?"

Certainly in the years leading up to Julian's final departure into professional care I had little time to do more than concentrate on her care and look after the daily housekeeping. I had to be continually thinking ahead to avoid situations that might cause her agitation or distress, and to fill up the day with occupations that would help her towards some enjoyment and serenity. It was helpful to have some task of my own to turn to in the brief hours when Julian was being cared for by someone else or when she slept, and I was able to write a short book on the question of the inspiration of the New Testament that was published in 2012 (*Is Scripture Still "Holy"?*). I found ways also to continue preaching and taking services regularly in our parish church — Julian was surprisingly content to come with me, though she seemed to have little sense of what was going on. So I contrived to keep my brain alert, even though our daily conversation no longer had any genuine content. But for any deeper spiritual searching or reflection the energy simply was not there, and I felt an almost culpable indifference to any of the great questions of life and death, of God and reality. Indeed at times it was this indifference, this apparent deadening of spiritual awareness, that caused me, and still causes me, anxiety and remorse. Now that I have more leisure, it should be possible to deepen my thinking, but I shall have to learn to do so. I am still plagued by a puritanical conscience about time — that I ought to be using every hour of it for some purpose that is of use to someone or something. I have often been told that, in my eighties, I should take advantage of my opportunities for genuine leisure without a sense of guilt; a wise use of leisure could bring, not only a greater awareness of myself and my resources, but a spiritual deepening capable of restoring to me some confidence in the truth of the Christian religion, for which I have always instinctively felt both loyalty and affection.

At the beginning of this account of my life I asked the question, "A gifted amateur?" There was certainly giftedness: one of my former students referred in a letter to my "Olympian intellect," and when I challenged him he was able (at least in his own mind) to justify the description. But it was a double-edged giftedness. Those who reach the highest level in their accomplishments normally concentrate on just one skill or pursuit. In my case there were too many gifts for me to perfect any one of them, too many ways to travel. Music in my case was never intended to be anything but amateur, though it remained a source of great pleasure, untinged by remorse that I did not achieve much technical competence. Academic ability I certainly had; but this was always hampered by an urge to use other gifts of which I was conscious, and which I felt I must bring into play for the good of others. As I have said, it was far too long before I realized that the profession of teaching and seeking to open the minds of young people could be as fulfilling and useful as any other occupation; and when I was a full-time academic I was made restless by the stirring of other gifts, particularly my abilities as an organizer and leader, and my talent for public speaking, lecturing, and preaching. It was this, perhaps, that had led me into ordination and a ministry that I attempted to combine with academic work; and this that prevented me from achieving real professionalism in either.

But a certain amateurishness in the use of the gifts I have been given is only one of the strands that need to be woven into an account of my life. Another was my continuing love affair with Julian and the influence she had on my character. I have described some of the dissonance that existed between my upbringing and hers, and the struggle that ensued between my instincts for a well-ordered and logical progress through life and her creative and sometimes (it seemed) subversive spontaneity. It is possible, I think, that apart from her I might have risen to the top of either of my professions — have become a professor or a bishop; and I know that some of my friends took this view, and wondered at the priority I gave to her needs, especially during the periods of her depression. But the question never presented itself to me in this way. Throughout our married life I remained very much in love with her, and any deliberate failure to give all I could to her and our family would have seemed inconceivable. But I was also profoundly conscious of what she had given to me in the way of an education in manners, sensitivity, and consideration for others. She could not do much about the abrasiveness that I was capable of when others were arguing with me or showing what I thought was a lack of good sense: this was a failing I had to deal with myself, and it is only recently that I have been able to notice a softening and mellowing in my manner, a greater ability to suffer fools gladly. But she continued to influence and challenge me by her extraordinary sensitivity to the needs and feelings of others, her exceptional courtesy and grace in her social manners, and her startling ability to seek out the meek and raise them in their own estimation. She once rebuked a canon's wife at Westminster Abbey for standing in the front row and preventing a worthy volunteer from having sight of a royal visitor — an episode that became firmly lodged in the memory of our family who witnessed it, all of whom she had imbued with the same sensitivity and concern for the stranger and the diffident. She also had an unerring intuition of the character of those she met, and could warn me of anyone who might be untrustworthy or malicious. I always listened carefully to her judgments and seldom found them mistaken. Indeed her capacity for intuitive judgment endured even in her dementia.

Along with the enormous gain that I derived from close contact with such a gifted and original person, there was of course also loss. Julian's world had in a way failed to move on from that of her parents' generation, and many aspects of modern life she found not merely uncongenial but alien. Her extreme sensitivity to any form of heartlessness or rudeness, and the danger that this would edge her further into withdrawal or depression, made me perhaps over-protective of her. It also made it difficult for her to share the hopes and aspirations of her children — hence her harsh judgment of them when they seemed not to be rising to her own standards of behavior; and this, as I have said, placed a strain on family life once they were adult, which I was often unable to alleviate. In later life I fell into the way of concealing from her some events or some encounters that I knew would upset her, and it may be that in so doing I made it still harder for her to come to terms with the realities of modern life. These included the many occasions on which I could not be available to her when she felt she needed me, and tempted me down a path of uxoriousness that could be open to criticism; yet at other times her life as a painter, and her delight in contemplating nature and rendering it in poetry or vivid prose, gave her an independence which in turn released me from caring for her. I was able to develop an ability to write and study despite frequent interruptions when she demanded my attention, and her resourcefulness in making use of her own time (when she did *not* like to be interrupted) gave me long periods entirely to myself. Our life together amidst the demands of my work and the pressure of social engagements and hospitality fell into a pattern of compromise between our different needs, which enabled me to fulfill the various roles which my work imposed on me, and gave her the independence she needed to use her own talents, even if at times she felt imprisoned by the routine imposed on her. Without her, I might have achieved more in worldly terms; but the lasting value of it would certainly have been less, and my character would not have received the honing which our life together made possible.

The third strand — my religious doubting — is much more subtly interwoven, and has necessarily remained hidden from all but a very few. It arises particularly from the one area in which I can say I have achieved a real professionalism. This is the preaching and pastoral work of a priest. I know that my sermons have often been received with gratitude and admiration, and I have found words to say to the bereaved, the doubting, and the sick which have elicited sometimes startling expressions of gratitude and appreciation. But in all of this I had a nagging sensation that I was not so much a priest, that is, a genuine interpreter and mediator of the things of God to human beings and of human hopes and needs to God, as a performer. For my public speaking and preaching I had a good delivery and a talent for clear exposition and argument, my style of writing was often commended for its elegance and clarity, and I was able to use words appropriate to pastoral situations in a way that was evidently found helpful; moreover I was always conscious of the enormous privilege enjoyed by the priest in being able to stand so close to people in moments of great significance in their lives — love and marriage, birth and baptisms, suffering and bereavement. But was it more than a performance? When I left the pulpit or the sufferer's bedside, had I done more than utter the appropriate words in a suitable tone of voice? Were my prayers for others anything more than a dutiful fulfillment of others' expectations of a priest? These were all performances that I carried out dutifully, and with the satisfaction that comes of any task well done. Yet I often could not help wondering whether it was all show, whether my apparent professionalism had simply blinded me to the fact that I did not have the resources of faith and spiritual depth that were needed to make them real. There was, of course, always satisfaction in performance itself — as any actor or musician knows. But I could not repress doubts about whether it was an authentic fruit of the Christian religion or merely the use of the gifts which, for various reasons, I have learned to exercise to others' apparent advantage. And these doubts remain with me to this day.

I used to put a question to my students who were preparing for ordination. Suppose, when you die, you meet a figure at the pearly gates whom you expect to be St. Peter (but who does not look quite like him), and request admission. Suppose he answers (in a kind but slightly superior manner) that he regrets you have been taken in all this time. "This Christian story on which you have based your life is, of course, quite without foundation. This Jesus whom you have believed in and have been proclaiming was deluded if he really thought he was the Son of God, and his followers seem to have been equally deluded ever since. I am afraid it is all nonsense really." What would be your reaction? Would you say, "Oh, if only I had known, I might have led my life quite differently"? Or would you feel that actually it did not make that much difference? Was not the Christian life so obviously the right one, the teaching of Jesus so clearly self-authenticating, the examples of service, courage, and hope given by his followers so inspiring, that no alternative course of life, no other moral and social priorities, could ever have seemed more challenging or more rewarding? And so it has seemed to me. And if, when I come to die, I am still agnostic even to the point of doubting the existence of God, I shall not be greatly disturbed, since I dare to hope that I have been true, at least, to my father's prediction that, as a priest, I would probably do less harm than good; and I believe I have also retained that residue of genuine religion which is implicit in those words I have quoted from Graham Greene's play, "I sometimes doubt my disbelief." Indeed, those few friends and advisers with whom I have shared any of these concerns about myself have encouraged me to think that even this small residue of faith may still mature into a perception and an experience of the transcendent which, stripped of conventional religious language and labored rationalization, may bring me gratefully to acknowledge that what has motivated the greater part of my life has been real — the reality of God.

Some Writings of Julian Harvey

Section 1: This account of her mother's early life was written by Julian many years after Jane's death.

My mother had left Oxford, deeply imbued by Maud Clark's sharing and teaching (Maud was only 7 years older than her). She was studying history, medieval especially, and she was to remain in Oxford deep in the complications of paleography. And then she was asked to begin the task of editing the Hamilton Papers. Her great friend at Somerville had been Flora Grierson, and she (Jane) was to be in Edinburgh with her father and mother (the mother with warmth and sense, the father Lord Rector of the University, alive, amusing, deeply into his own poetry and research).

It was one of those tall, old, spacious houses that looked on to Arthur's Seat, grass-covered and superb, the whole house beautiful and welcoming. Herbert himself was there at the station, distinguished, tall, in his old rambling car, talking hard. "Jane — I will call you that, if I may? — I've found a little place that makes wonderful scones. It's tea time. Stay a moment and I'll run in and get them."

People came — yet always there was a sense of peace. The daughters (he had five) would go to their art and their music, worried only by the eldest, whose beloved fiancé had died and whom they had to entice, despite her tears, to the church she so loved. She was beautiful and a poet.

Breakfast was a wonderful time, before she went off to her

own work. W. B. Yeats was a great friend, and would often stop for a night on his way. They (he and Herbert Grierson) would talk, and the talk would go between them of writers, of the written, of poetry and of Ireland. And all those friends had in common the laughter and the vividness of St. John Gogarty.... But it was real, slipping naturally into poetry and into what mattered (what they rebelled against and what they cared for — "as you would for seeds," his wife would add.)

Herbert Grierson did on rare occasions suffer from the gloom that was so prevalent and seemed natural in the country of his birth, the Shetlands. Occasionally my mother would remember his saying to his wife, "Why did we bear five pledges to fortune?" But she would smile kindly, and he would lose it in one of those great walks right to the top of Arthur's Seat. And she would talk to the three lovely helpers from the Shetlands, who were so completely part of the house (they told my mother how to wash wool so as to recover the wool's gentleness and discard the unneeded grease: "You do it quickly with hot water, that's it"). They were a joy, all three.

My mother loved Yeats coming. To her he had given those two lovely books of his poems, inscribed carefully. He told her of his 'tower.' "We saved it. It's not very high, and you sleep in a room (one on each floor) and in the morning early, or if the moon is out, you can watch the water going all on its own, and if you are still the otters will come. Oh, it is peace itself. I would love you to come and stay. My wife would too (she's a bit of a mystic, I think). Will you? I'll write and tell you how to come. No, I mean it."

She was thrilled. And she knew he meant it. She had heard him so often chanting those poems he so loved; and into the chanting came the place he longed for, with his Ireland and its peace. She would hear it from quiet room to quiet room. She knew the poems now, with the timeless rhythm that he used.

I will arise and go now, go to Innisfree,
And a small cabin built there, of clay and wattles made;
Nine bean rows will I build there, a hive for the honey-bee,
And live alone in the bee-loud glade....

He was off then, and for a much longer time, for he had to talk, many times, and it was 'goodbye' then.

"Herbert," he said, "when I am down there at the station, waiting for the train and having a drink of that fine clear water from one of the fine metal cups, I'll be writing a poem, but thinking of you, climbing Arthur's seat."

But my mother had to go home, to a tiny house and her difficult mother. Her beloved father had died at the end of her very first term at Oxford. He had left her himself with the Principal saying, "When you've finished it all, we'll go painting together — perhaps to the West Indies."

No letter came to the small Cotswold village. She was so certain Yeats would write. He had meant it, she knew. "What a fuss," her mother said, "Lost in the post, I expect." There was only one very small old shop, a Post Office, in the village. Julia, with white hair and jet black frocks, always gossipy and grumpy, ruled it. Alas, when the letter turned up (her mother had got it from Julia) it was much too late. She had to go back to Edinburgh now. "Well, how could you afford it anyway?" her mother said, oblivious of her tears.

Section 2: *Something of the flavor of Jerusalem in the 1960s is conveyed by Julian's account of one of her experiences.*

One of my favourite ways in the Old City was the steep narrow street of the Via Dolorosa. Perhaps, at first, it was somewhat daunting, and its narrowness made it more so, particularly because people still spoke of Pope Pius VI's pilgrimage. The crowds there to greet him had been so thick down this narrow street that he had been forced (not through cowardice, but for mere survival) to escape into one of the houses to recover.

The first place I discovered here was the long, low shop of the Little Sisters of Charles de Foucault. In their rough blue serge and bare sandalled feet they would be selling the pottery some of them had made: delicate figures, of Mary looking down at her child, and Joseph, tall and quietly wondering. They were of terra cotta, and as simple, and as quick and essential, as the Sisters who made them. The Sisters kept the Sixth Station of the Cross, where Veronica is said to have wiped the face of Christ. It was good to stop there to pray, as many did, unobtrusively.

On the other side, a little higher up, was an Armenian Pottery, and the Armenian potter himself. How I delighted in the things he had made. His ancestors had come from Armenia several centuries ago to replace, renew, and work on, the beautiful old tiles that decorated much of the outside of the Dome of the Rock. A few of those very skilled men, with their families, had stayed on, handing down their skills from one generation to another. One of the first things I bought (a present for my husband) was a solid rectangular tile representing part of the Madaba Map, the sixth century mosaic set in the floor of the church in the village of that name. It was a map of Aelia Capitolina, the new city of Jerusalem built by the Romans (we could go and see a pillar that remained from the main street, in a shop in the old city, by courtesy of those who worked there). On another of my visits he had displayed about ten tiles. They were large and unlike anything I had seen. They glowed and were full of sunshine. They were a series of minarets, each delicate and alive. The landscape, desert-scape, round them was golden too, though the minarets were paler and quieter in colour. "No, I did not do them. They are the work of our Jordanian painter. He works in Beirut now." Often I would go to look at them — they were hard to leave.

But to return to the Little Sisters. Through my delight in their figures, through the peace and quiet in their chapel, and through a growing realization of their own goodness I began to know them a little. Alone, of all the inhabitants of the Via Dolorosa, they had a room which stretched across it, bridge-like, and, like much of the street, old, unobtrusive, and in this case beautiful. Hearing that I was hoping to paint a little, they said I could do it from the window in their room, the one directly over the Via Dolorosa! They only used it, they said, if many were coming, or for a rare reception. It had one of those intricate wooden shutters — "good to see through" which, in the past, ladies could see from without being seen. I could easily open it, they said, if I wanted more light; from below, no one would notice me at all! Their peace pervaded the room. No one came near me. I could look down that narrow street, each house a building that was a little different from its neighbour. Below me, on my left, the sign of the Armenian potter over his small entrance; on my right, people disappearing to say a prayer at the Veronica shrine.

I first came to this room on a day when it was raining, so I dared to open the close-fitting wooden lattice of the shutter. I could see the rain shining on the cobbles. Presently a tall Arab, his black umbrella held high, walked slowly up the middle of the street; his large umbrella caught the light so that part of it shone white, like the cobble stones. That he was alone, with the different buildings beside and behind him, made the age of the street and its ancient, and sometimes added-to buildings, more defined. It gave a new perspective: some buildings were rounded, or built out a little, as if in rivalry. How had this single Arab, walking upright and alone, with the whiteness of the rain on his black umbrella in an otherwise empty street, made the Via Dolorosa, for ever, entirely different for me?

Considerably later on, we were at the Easter ceremony of the Holy Fire in the Church of the Holy Sepulchre, with many pilgrims from all over the world. Anthony was on the ground among the crowds, where everyone had their bunch of tall, thin candles waiting for the Holy Fire to come out from the Sepulchre. I, more fortunate, was on a balcony above the crowds. It was easy to see from there. In the long wait, I grew fascinated by the "poor Copts," come from Egypt, worried and weary, in their long, torn clothes. Many were perched up on the heavy metal scaffolding against the walls of this part of the church. They were the poorest of the pilgrims and had often walked much of the way. I did a quick, hidden pencil sketch of them waiting on the far side, some way below me, each one resting against the tall scaffolding that was in the shape of the St Andrew's Cross. Tired, with their eyes shut, each clasping their bunch of candles tightly — might not one of them fall?

Later I took the sketch to the Armenian potter, Stepan Karakashian (I had been told his name by now). Yes, he said, he could put it on a tile, draw it on, and he would add some of the original blue in their robes. "It is not difficult," he said. He was like that! And much,

much later (we had left Jerusalem ten days before the June War in 1967 and had already been back in England for three or four months) I was amazed, and deeply humbled, when a carefully packed parcel containing four heavy tiles of my sketch arrived! I never knew how it had come or who had brought it. And how clearly he had written on it the Greek words (suggested by Anthony) meaning WAKE, THOU THAT SLEEPEST.

Principal Publications

1970   *Companion to the New Testament* (New English Bible), Oxford
        University Press & Cambridge University Press (Second Edi-
        tion, Cambridge University Press 2004)
1975   *Priest or President?* London: SPCK
1976   *Jesus on Trial: A Study in the Fourth Gospel* London: SPCK
1977   *Something Overheard: An Introduction to the New Testament* Lon-
        don: Bible Reading Fellowship
1981   (Ed.) *God Incarnate: Story and Belief* London: SPCK
1982   *Jesus and the Constraints of History* (The Bampton lectures 1980)
        London: Duckworth
1984   *Believing and Belonging: The Practice of Believing in the Church* Lon-
        don: SPCK
1985   (Ed.) *Alternative Approaches to New Testament Study* London:
        SPCK
1990   *Retaliation: A Political and Strategic Option under Moral and Reli-
        gious Scrutiny* London: Council on Christian Approaches to
        Defence and Disarmament
1990   *Strenuous Commands: The Ethic of Jesus* London: SCM Press
1994   *Promise or Pretence? A Christian's Guide to Sexual Morals* London:
        SCM Press
1995   *Renewal through Suffering: A Study of 2 Corinthians* Edinburgh:
        T&T Clark
1996   *Marriage, Divorce and the Church* London: Darton, Longman
        and Todd

1999   *Demanding Peace: Christian Responses to War and Violence* London:
        SCM Press

2001   *By What Authority? The Churches and Social Concern* London:
        SCM Press

2008   (Translated) *Elias Chacour: Faith Beyond Despair* Norwich:
        Canterbury Press

2009   *Asylum in Britain: A Question of Conscience* Humanitas: The Jour-
        nal of the George Bell Institute

2012   *Is Scripture Still Holy?: Coming of Age with the New Testament*
        Grand Rapids, Michigan: William B. Eerdmans

Index of Names and Places

Index of Names and Places

Istanbul, 64
Italy, 7, 25, 157

Japan, Emperor and Empress of, 105-106
Jerusalem, 56ff., 157
John, Esther, 113, 114
John of the Cross, Saint, 135, 152
Jukes, Fr. John, 81

King, Martin Luther, 112, 113
King's College London, 66, 72
Kinshasa, 136, 137, 140, 141, 142
Kinsman, Tommy, 47
Kitangu, prophet, 138
Knapp-Fisher, Bishop Edward, 117
Kolbe, Maximilian, 113
Krätschel, Werner, 103

LAMDA, 153
Lanfranc, Archbishop, 72
La Pira, Giorgio, 13
Laurentian Library, 13
Lawrence of Arabia, 58
Leach, Bernard, 79
Lelli, Mr ('Pretini'), 25
Lermontov, 3
Leonardo, 26
Leopold II, King, 142
Lloyd-Jones, Hugh, 53
Lorraine, 6
Luwum, Archbishop Janani, 113

MacInnes, Archbishop Campbell, 56, 59, 60
McKisick, Miss, 24
McMaster, Ian, 14
McMaster, Jane, 14, 28
Mandela, Nelson, 106
Marina, Princess, 44
Martini, Simone, 26
Masemola, Manche, 113, 117
Mannering, General, 25, 27
Markey, Sister Hilary, 116
Maycock, Hugh, 74
Mayne, Dean Michael, 110, 116

Mindszenty, Cardinal,
Milhaud, Darius, 158
Mobutu, President, 137, 138
Monique, Soeur, 144
Montegufoni, 27
Morris, Canon Alun, 56, 62
Munich, 11, 12, 14, 16, 31, 32, 33, 34, 36, 37
Murray, Gilbert, 53, 63

Namur, 6
Naples, Bay of, 65
Nazis, 8, 10
Neary, Martin, 123-124
Nelson, Horatio, 131
Neville, Mary, 92-93
Nevis, 131-133
New York, 49
Nouwen, Henri, 162
Nuffield Hospital, 8

O'Brien, Sir Richard, 119
Odysseus, 157
Oxford: city, 2, 8, 23, 24, 157; Queens'
  College, 18, 86; Somerville College, 18,
  24; University Church, 40; Wolfson
  College, 86; Worcester College, 8, 91,
  153

Paris, 153, 157, 164
Pfeiffer, Rudolf, 10
Piachaud, François, 46, 100
Pogson, John, 130
Poliziano, 26
Ponsar, Alain, 78
Powell, Enoch, 18
Pushkin, 3
Pym, Barbara, 127

Queens' (The Queens' College), 18, 86,
  87, 94
Qumran, 57

Raphaël (Mpanzu), 136-142
Raskin, Maurice, 2, 5, 6
Roberts, Colin, 54